Upper Chesapeake Bay Decoys And Their Makers

David and Joan Hagan

Schiffer Publishing Ltd
1469 Morstein Road, West Chester, Pennsylvania 19380

Thanks

Canada Geese climb skyward.

This book could not have been successful without help of many fine and wonderful people. We would like to thank the collectors who so graciously offered us the opportunity to photograph the decoys of the deceased makers from their collections. We would like to thank all the decoy makers and game wardens who have endured our questions and many photo sessions. As outsiders to the decoy world, we have made many cherished friends and have gained in knowledge of a true American folk art.

Special Thanks to those people, whose help was invaluable in contributing to this effort.

Betty Jean Brown, Bob Coleman, Bob Faul, Richard Gill, Donna Grove, Havre De Grace Decoy Museum, Somers Headley, Bob Litzenberg, Jimmy Pierce, John Simon, Dick Shaffer, and Bill Veasey

Dedication

We dedicate this book to William "Bill" Veasey and Donna Grove, for giving us the chance to grow and share.

Cover photo: Guide Gerry Haggerty sets Canada Goose v-boards before hunt on Langford Creek off the Chester River.

Title page photo: Canada Geese feeding in snow.

Library of Congress Catalog Number: 90-60738.

Printed in the United States of America.
ISBN: 0-88740-258-5

Published by Schiffer Publishing, Ltd.
1469 Morstein Road
West Chester, Pennsylvania 19380
Please write for a free catalog.
This book may be purchased from the publisher.
Please include $2.00 postage.
Try your bookstore first.

Mallard drake.

Contents

November 20, 1989

David and Joan Hagan
Golden Memories Studio
2413 Harkins Road
White Hall, MD 21161

Dear David and Joan

I am pleased that you have focused your artistic talents on the waterfowl of Maryland and the Chesapeake Bay area. We are blessed, indeed, to have such an abundance of nautral resources in this area, and among the most treasured are the waterfowl of the bay.

Carving and painting decoys has become a very respected art form. It is supported and encouraged by the state and other government agencies, and adds a great deal to the cultural diversity of Maryland. The artistic talent and craftsmanship that goes into carving and painting decoys makes them very valuable to serious collectors.

Please accept my best wishes for a very successful venture in the publication of these photographs showing the fine work of decoy makers in the Chesapeake Bay region.

Sincerely,

William Donald Schaefer

Governor

Governor of Maryland "William Donald Shaefer"

Introduction

The making hunting decoys is one of the true American folk arts. From simple forms carved out of scraps of timber to intricately painted, highly detailed art pieces, the decoy represents the creative insight and skill of the carver and painter.

In the days of the market hunters, decoys were roughly made. Just the basic colors of the hunted species were used. Painted wing feathers and eyes were not common, because such details were not important to bring ducks into gunning range.

Now decoys are made with much more care and attention to detail. While hunters still use them, they do not use them in as great a number. Instead, a growing number of decoys go to collectors, those who appreciate the art and beauty they possess. While the collector is interested in the old decoy and their makers, they also collect new decoys, decoys that will never see the water.

The decoys in *Decoys and their Makers of the Upper Chesapeake Bay* include both old and new, those made for hunting and those made for collecting. It includes many examples of both in full color as well as the colorful stories of the people who made them.

To gather this information, the same questions were asked of each living decoy maker to keep the text uniform. Three of the decoy makers have passed away since we began photographing in 1982. Their stories were told to us by close family members. The stories are transcribed from our conversations with makers or their relatives and are presented as they were told to us. As you will see, there is no doubt that there were more ducks killed in the stories told in various decoy shops then were ever killed out on the flats.

The decoy makers in this area have enriched Maryland's history with their talents and with their commitment and spirit to keep the art of decoy making alive in a changing world. Every one of the younger decoy makers will tell you that all they have to do is ask for help and the older guys are only too glad to do so.

Dave has had the opportunity to hunt waterfowl while body booting on the flats. Standing in the water of the Susquehanna Flats up to your chest in water is one thing. When the water is freezing on your gun and you hands are so cold you cannot move them, is quite another. It is an experience that every hardy waterfowl hunter should be able to say he did once. We have hunted and photographed waterfowl over decoys made from automobile tires, plastic, card board, wood and taxidermist mounted birds called "stuffers".

The hard work of setting out decoys in the bitter cold before daylight is for those most serious about the sport. Not getting a shot or, even worse, not seeing anything fly by all day, only helps to make the cold seem colder when you pick up the decoys at sunset. Yet when you are in the company of your friends on such trips, the stories seem always to have a better ending.

The area we covered for material is limited to the western and eastern shore surrounding the Chesapeake Bay from the Chesapeake Bay Bridge north. *Decoys and their Makers of the Upper Chesapeake Bay* is designed to show the decoy styles in this area as far back as possible while bringing you into the methods of hunting waterfowl in the 1990s. We would like for you to get to know this great group of people a little better through their stories.

If we have missed mentioning anyone, it most certainly was not done purposely and we must apologize. We hope you enjoy reading this book as much as we enjoyed doing it.

Authors and photographers David and Joan Hagan. Photo taken by Ernie Preston.

Makers

Carroll "Wally" Algard
Born: 1883 lived in Charlestown, Cecil County, Maryland
Died: 1959

Charles N. Barnard
Born: 1876 lived in Havre De Grace, Harford County, Maryland
Died: 1958

Canvasback hen by Carroll "Wally" Algard.

Blackhead drake by Charles N. Barnard.

Canvasback drake by Mr. Barnard.

George W. "Wash" Barnes
Born: 1861 lived in Carpenter's Point, Cecil County, Maryland
Died: 1915

Canvasback hen by George Washington "Wash" Barnes.

Samuel "Sam" Barnes
Born: 1847 lived in Havre De Grace, Harford County, Maryland
Died: 1926

Canvasback drake by Samuel "Sam" Barnes.

Clarence F. "Tit Bird" Bauer

"I was born in Havre de Grace in 1924 and completed nine years of schooling. I worked for the government at Aberdeen Proving Ground until I retired in 1970.

"When I was six years old I got interested in watching Jim Currier make decoys in his shop. I started fooling with them then and have never stopped. I worked part time in Mitchell's shop for near thirty-two years. After I retired I went to work for Madison full time. When he sold his shop in 1979 to Bill Collins I started full time for myself.

"I make full size birds, half size and miniatures. The miniatures make up the majority of my work now days. My painting and body styles haven't changed much over the years. I use white pine and bass wood for the bodies and I still paint with oil base paints.

"All of the miniatures are cut out on a bandsaw and the full bodies are machine turned. I do all the work by myself and have made thousands of decoys.

"Gunning on the flats as a teenager just seemed natural in those days. I've gunned the body boots, but I bushwhacked the most till I gave it up. Elmer Simpers and Doc Chambers gunned with me most of the time. One time in 1978 Doc Chambers, Elmer Simpers and me were bushwhacking on the flats around two o'clock in the afternoon when it started to snow. We had put out about a hundred Canvasback decoys and started to row back toward the John Goose. Elmer Simpers was watching the ducks land in the rig. It was coming down so hard we could hardly see the John Goose. We made one scull into the decoys, slapped the side of the boat with the sculling oar and the ducks jumped up to give us good shooting. They just kept coming and landing in the decoys as we were trying to pick up the dead birds. We just stayed there in the decoys shooting till we shot every shell we had on board. In about a half hour we had killed one hundred and one Canvasbacks."

Clarence "Tit Bird" Bauer painting Mallard drake miniature with full-size Mallard drake in foreground.

Miniature decoys by Mr. Bauer. Clockwise from top right: Pintail drake, Red-breasted Merganser drake, Canvasback hen, Mallard drake, Ruddy Duck drake, Blackhead drake, Blackhead hen, Ruddy Duck hen, Mallard hen, Canvasback drake, Red-breasted Merganser hen, Pintail hen. Center, Whistling (Tundra) Swan.

George David "Dave" Blackiston, Jr.

"I was born August 18, 1928 in Chestertown, Maryland. After school I started to work in the printing business. I work for a news paper locally as a composition manager.

"I started making decoys to gun over in 1940 or '41. We used the old square antifreeze cans. They were painted flat black and were used for Black ducks. We would tie the string and weight to the metal handle on the top of the can and throw them over. I gunned with Danny Peterson and Matthew Walsh.

"After I was discharged from the service in 1952 my brother and Speedy Joiner were working for the Chestertown light company. My brother talked me into going over to Speed's shop and make a few decoys to start gunning over. We made some Redheads and Blackheads. Speedy showed us what to do, since we didn't know the first thing about it. The first mistake I made was to cut all the blocks an inch too short. He turned them out on his machine with his pattern. Till this day if Speedy sees one of those decoys he knows it was one of those short blocks.

"In 1953 I started gunning with Mr. Ed Robinson at Quaker Neck. There were two Black duck blinds and one diving duck blind on Hollow Marsh. Mr. Ed used Heverin decoys. In 1918 or '29 he had taken a bunch of blocks to Heverin. Heverin hand chopped those blocks into decoys for twenty cents a piece. Those decoys would not stay upright in the water all of the time. You would go out to turn one upright and knock several others over. So in 1955 Mr. Ed talked to Charlie Joiner and made a deal with him. Speedy told Mr. Ed that he would make him a new decoy in trade for every old one of Heverin's. It was then that decoy collecting started to take off. Mr. Ed wound up with about one hundred Canvasbacks and ten Whifflers or Golden

George David "Dave" Blackiston, Jr. with Green-winged Teal drake in paint room.

Top, Green-winged Teal hen. Bottom, Green-winged Teal drake made by Dave Blackiston.

Eyes as most people know them. The Whifflers never were put overboard. I should have bought them when we quit gunning but I didn't. Just one of the mistakes I made in my time.

"I had just about quit gunning after Mr. Ed passed away. There was a guy by the name of Doug Wallace who asked me to go gunning with him in 1984. Well I went with him and had a good time. The decoys he had were rubber and plastic. Some of them were half-sunk or didn't float right. I told him that I thought I could make a better looking decoy than what he had there. He said, 'Do it.' I bought some cork and made Black duck and Mallard decoys for us. Of course I would take then to Speedy to look at and see if I was okay on this or that. He said, "Your decoys look okay, but you have got to get away from that cork. It is bad for your lungs, your body can't expel it from your lungs." I switched over to wood at that time.

"Speedy gave me a Green Wing Teal pattern that he never used. It's the only one I have ever made. It has won me several ribbons in competitions and I can't keep up with the orders for it.

"Mr. Charlie Joiner is one of the finest men to walk the face of the earth. He is very congenial, he does not know the meaning of the word no. He will stop work in his shop and come over to your shop to help you with a problem. My decoys are influenced by him both in style and in paint. I use the same movements as he does when painting. You start at the back of the bird and move forward, painting the eyes and bill last. If you are painting more than one species of birds at one time, and you are painting black, you paint the black where it goes on all the birds. When you start with a color you paint everything with that color at one time. I try to put a little more detail in the side pockets and the bill then Speedy does. I try to make it look a little different than his.

"Bass wood is the primary wood I use. I paint with tube oils and Rustoleum. When I first started out I bought brushes like a fisherman will buy fishing lures. After a while you will find out you only need about five different brushes. All the birds I cut out are flat bottom. When I make round bottom birds I have someone turn the bodies for me."

I have probably made around a thousand decoys or so. My wife comes out and helps to put on the paint sealer from time to time. I'm making fifty-three Blackhead round bottom gunning decoys from Speedy's pattern right now. I intend to gun them this year with Stan Wallace at Madison Bay in Dorchester County.

"We used to put out two hundred pounds of corn out three times a week. We shot Mondays, Wednesdays and Saturdays. It was an unwritten law on the Chester River, you gunned those three days only. Most times we shot from half-hour before sun-up till about nine o'clock in the morning. At the end of the hunt we would put out the corn. There was an old wooden fish box that we put on the front of the boat. The two hundred pound sacks of corn were dumped into that. Mr. Ed and I would each take a bailer and throw a scoop to the left then to the right for about twenty-five yards wide and forty-five yards long. This was done when it was legal to put bait no closer to the blind then two hundred yards. We fed Black ducks all during the year, but only shot them three times a season, when the bay got rough and the wind blew at least thirty-five miles per hour. It took that kind of weather to drive them into the coves."

John Blair, Jr.
Born: 1881 lived in Blairs Shore, Cecil County, Maryland
Died: 1953

Black Duck by John Blair, Jr.

Blackhead drake by Mr. Blair.

John Blair, Sr.
Born: 1842 lived in Blairs Shore, Cecil County, Maryland
Died: 1927

Blackhead drake by John Blair, Sr.

Pintail drake by John Blair Sr.

Blue-winged Teal drake by Mr. Blair.

Bryan Bodt

"I was born May 25, 1963 in Baltimore, Maryland. I graduated from Bel Air High School, then attended Washington College in Chestertown, Maryland where I got my Bachelor of Science Degree in Biology.

"I am a self-employed decoy maker. After I completed my schooling I started in making the decoys. Actually I started making decoys long before I finished college. If I remember correctly it was about 1977. It began as a hobby because of my interest in waterfowl hunting. The first things I made were heads. You could say my enthusiasm was sparked by my father's interest in antique decoys and hunting in the Havre de Grace area.

"In the early 1980s I spent about three years working for Jim Pierce. You could say he had a big influence in my style of carving. Also, Paul Gibson, Madison Mitchell and Charlie Bryan were contributing factors in my work. But, like most carvers, I wanted to develop my own style. I carve the hen and drake of about 15 species of ducks. The Canada Goose, Snow Goose, Blue Goose and Swan are the larger birds that I make.

"I use different woods for my carvings. For the bodies I use white cedar, white pine and tupelo. For the heads it's mainly sugar pine.

"Most of the paints I use are home-mixed based on Rustoleum and Japan color pigments. Most birds average five coats of paint, 1 varnish, 2 undercoat or primer, 1 base color and 1 topcoat.

"The tools I use are the standard tools of the trade. That is a spoke shave, draw knives, band saws, pneumatic sanders, belt sander and a decoy lathe. The lathe I acquired in 1985. It was made by Alan Burdette and David Walker. The machine is typical of the type used around Havre de Grace.

"The bodies are machine turned. This requires a lot of 're-working' after turning. The heads are hand made.

"My father helps with the early stages (i.e.: cutting trees and 'blocking out') and with final paint. We paint using a 'wet-on-wet' technique, which is not in keeping with the Havre de Grace style.

"Most of my customers are collectors as opposed to gunners. Maybe one percent are gunners. It is much cheaper for the hunter to buy the plastic decoys.

"I have hunted on the Sassafras River and the Susquehanna Flats. I've never done body-booting. I do lay-out hunting. As far as I know, it is still legal.

"One hunt I remember was when we killed twelve ducks and they were of eleven different species. This was about two years ago on the Friday before Thanksgiving on the Sassafras River. It was raining to beat the band and it just drove everything through there.

Bryon Bodt nails head on Pintail body.

Canada Goose V-boards surround layout rig belonging to Bernie, Bryon Bodt, and Leonard Burcham on the Sassafras River in Cecil Co.

Bottom left clockwise, Ruddy Duck drake, Canvasback hen sleeper, Brant, Canvasback drake and Ruddy Duck hen.

Richard Charles Borden
Born: 1928 lived in Charlestown, Cecil County, Maryland
Died: 1987

Canvasback drake by Richard Charles Borden sitting on unfinished decoy body.

Redhead drake by Mr. Borden sitting on unfinished decoy body.

Taylor L. Boyd
Born: 1856 lived in Perryville, Cecil County, Maryland
Died: 1946

Canvasback drake by Taylor L. Boyd.

Charles "Charlie" Bryan

"I was born April 4, 1902 in Baltimore, Maryland. After I completed high school, I had four years at Maryland Institute. I took mechanical drawing. My full time profession was as a machinist.

"I started making decoys because I was too cheap to buy them and I wanted them. I was around 36 years old when I started.

"When I first saw Madison Mitchell's birds he became my biggest influence. And it goes without saying that when I saw Charlie Joiner's style of painting that became another influence. They made the biggest impression on me.

"I've used all different types of wood: cedar, pine, bass and some paulownia. Every once in a while I made maybe a handful out of mahogany or walnut.

"I use regular old oil base house paint.

"Some of the other materials I have used are cork and foam, and I have made some molds and patterns and cast them. I've also used polystyrene beads that you heated.

"All my decoys were machine made. The first ones I made I band-sawed a rough shape and then I worked them by hand. It wasn't long after that, that I built my own duplicator.

"I have made about two to three hundred decoys a year for the last thirty years. I've made Swan, goose, Brant, Snow Goose, Blue Goose, Canvasback, Redhead, Blackhead, Black Duck, Mallard, Coots, Sea gull, Teal, Bufflehead, Golden Eye, Ringneck, and cast iron wing ducks, to name a few. I've made a lot of silhouettes, both field decoys as well as V-boards for water decoys.

"I made my own machine. I found out Bob Harman, in Aberdeen, had a little duplicator. When I first started to turn decoys for myself I would go up to Bob and he would charge me ten cents a piece to run a body. My machine is basically his idea.

"When I first started making decoys I had never seen anybody actually make them. All I saw was the finished product. I didn't know how they did it, as far as holding the bird went. I saw the spoke shave knives in their shops, but it seemed that I happened to be there when they were painting. I wound up going to Sears and buying a cast iron draw knife. It wouldn't cut. So I took it down to my shop and I went to work on it. I filed it and relieved it inside. I threw the blade away and got a hacksaw blade. I got it to where I could cut with it. But then I realized I didn't know the how to hold it in a vise. I didn't have a vise, so I made a square piece like a shoemakers last. I fastened it to a column, put down the bottom of the bird, spoke shaved one end and picked it up , turned it a hundred and eighty degrees and spoke shaved the other end. I did all the bottoms of the birds first. Then when I turned them over, still nailed to that jig that I made, I would spoke shave, draw knife and then put the head on. When I took if off the fixture I would be ready to sand it.

"My boys helped me in my shop. At that time most of my decoys were cedar poles and they would help me do all the blocking. That consisted of using a sledge hammer and a wedge. When I made the silhouettes, the boys were in high school. They did practically everything but saw.

"One of the biggest changes I've made in my decoy making is in the head. Madison made two types of head. When they cut at the bill, they cut from the body into the bill. It's recessed at the head. When he cuts a decorative bird it's cut so that the bill sets up into the head. When I saw his decorative style I liked it. So all my decoys I make have the bill set up in the head like Madison's.

"I've sold a lot of decoys to National Sporting Goods. George Thompson (he owned Thompson's Seagirt House), he used my birds for gunning. Augie, who has a crab place in Edgemere, was also one of my customers.

"The Bald Pate would have to be my favorite species of duck. I've always had a soft spot in my heart for them. They were easy to pick and I never found one that had a foul odor or a bad taste.

"One of the things that made me feel the best was the time I had made some Bald Pates. Most of the carvers made the Bald Pate on a diving duck style. I felt the Bald Pate should be set up in the back end. His white should show on his butt. I made all my Bald Pates on a spring tail body. I happened to be going up to Madison's and I took it along with me. It just so happened he was by himself that day. I asked him what he thought of it. He told me it was mighty fine and he would like to have a hundred of them. It really made me feel good. I felt like I must be doing something right for Madison to okay it."

Charles "Charlie" Bryan puts finishing touch on Green-winged Teal drake. A pair of Charlie's Mallards hang in the background while another Green-winged Teal drake is drying in the foreground.

Charlie Bryan was named Honorary Chairman for the 1984 Havre de Grace Decoy Festival. Charles and his wife Anna pose next to the complete full-size collection that was sold at auction.

Redhead V-boards were the first decoys made by Charlie Bryan.

American Coot made by Mr. Bryan.

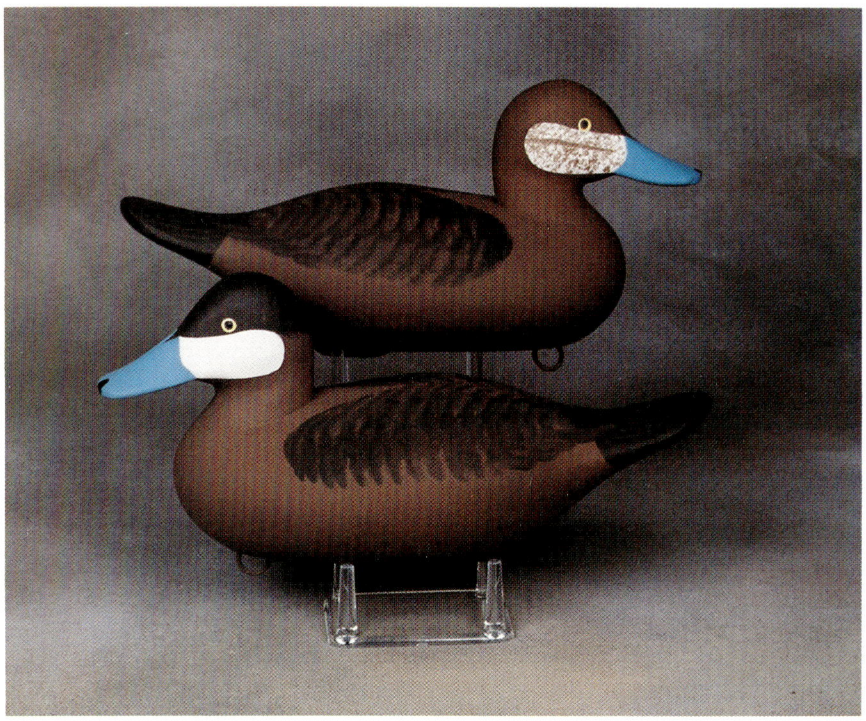

Top, Ruddy Duck hen. Bottom, Ruddy Duck drake made by Mr. Bryan.

Top, Redhead hen. Bottom, Redhead drake by Mr. Bryan.

Top, Mallard hen. Bottom, Mallard drake by Mr. Bryan.

Left, Goldeneye hen. Right, Goldeneye drake by Mr. Bryan.
Both decoys are flat bottom with wooden keel.

Top, Canvasback drake. Bottom, Canvasback hen sleeper by Mr. Bryan.

Whistling (Tundra) Swan with wooden keel in display stand made by Charlie Bryan.

Bufflehead hen by Mr. Bryan.

Top, Cast iron sinkbox decoy, Canvasback hen. Bottom, Cast iron sinkbox decoy, Canvasback drake by Mr. Bryan.

Canada Goose, flat bottom with wooden keel by Mr. Bryan.

Brant, flat bottom with wooden keel by Mr. Bryan.

Blue Goose, flat bottom with wooden keel.

Snow Goose, flat bottom with wooden keel.

Top, Black Duck. Bottom, Black Duck sleeper.

The only pair of White farm ducks that Charlie Bryan made. They were made as a gift for little children who had lost their pet ducks.

Top, Ringed-necked Duck hen. Bottom, Ringed-necked Duck drake by Charlie Bryan.

Top, Blackhead hen. Bottom, Blackhead drake by Mr. Bryan.

Top, Pintail hen. Bottom, Pintail drake by Mr. Bryan.

Sea Gull, used as confidence decoy by Charlie Bryan.

Top, American Widgeon (Baldpate) hen. Bottom, American Widgeon (Baldpate) drake by Mr. Bryan.

Top, flat bottom Mallard hen. Bottom, flat bottom Mallard drake. Decoys were made by Charlie Bryan and painted by Charlie Joiner. Only five pair like these exist.

Leonard Burcham is seen carving a duck head. Canada Goose in background, pair of Green-winged teal in foreground.

Leonard Burcham

"I was born February 4, 1938 in Baltimore, Maryland. At that time my parents were living in Emmorton, Maryland. The last twenty-three years I have lived in Havre de Grace, Maryland.

"I graduated from Bel Air High School, class of 1956.

"Most of my life I have been a laboratory technician with American Cyanamid Corporation.

"I always enjoyed gunning but the cost of decoys to buy was too expensive. I was just poor folk, so at the age of 35 I started to make my own.

"The person who had the biggest influence on my carving was Dick Hipple. He kind of got me set up in the business. He had a couple of silhouette patterns that he gave me and I just sort of took off from there. I messed around a little bit with Madison Mitchell but I wanted to have my own style early on and that's the reason I stayed with the hand-chopped block.

"I prefer to use white cedar for a gunning bird. I will work white pine and I have used some bass wood. I make a flat bottom decoy.

"I like to use artist oil paints with a little bit of Rustoleum thrown in.

"I don't have a machine. I blank everything out on a band saw and then I go right to draw knife and spoke shave. I don't even have a drum sander. Everything is hand-sanded.

"I have probably made between five and seven thousand decoys if I include the miniatures. I still gun over my gunning birds all though I don't do it as much as I would like to.

"People from all over the country (at least 22 states) and many foreign countries (at least 8) have purchased my decoys, men, women and children of all ages. Some of my more famous customers are The Library of Congress and The Future Homemakers of America.

"I still hunt, mainly the Susquehanna Flats, Sassafras River, and the Chesapeake Bay. I hunt with Bernie Bodt, Bryon Bodt, Larry Chapman, John Paxton, Jim Hooker, and Rick Grubb."

"One particular hunt comes to mind. It was three years ago on a November day with a northwest wind of about 10-15 m.p.h. and a slow but steady rain. We had laid out the rig with only a six man crew. We elected to put three men in to gun with two on stand-by to pick up downed birds and one man to remain on the cabin boat. However, the ducks had different ideas. We very quickly put a fourth man in to gun. That morning everyone was wet to the skin but nobody gave that a second thought, as this was a day we would long talk about as one of our most successful hunts."

The decoys by Leonard Burcham are, top left, Canvasback hen. Top right, Canvasback drake. Left middle, Blackhead drake. Right middle, Blackhead hen. Left front, Mallard hen. Right front, Mallard drake.

Daniel "Danny" Carson

I was born on June 20, 1966. Havre de Grace in Harford County is where I was raised and go to school. I went to John Carrol High School and am attending Harford Community College full-time now. I plan to attend Delaware University after that.

"I used to work on a horse farm near Jim Pierce's shop. I would just stop by every now and then, and I guess I got hooked. Since I liked to hunt it was interesting to me from the start.

"It was 1981 when I began making decoys at Pierce's. Jim Pierce has taught me all the fundamentals of decoy making that he himself learned from Mr. Mitchell. When I have my own shop someday I plan to change some of the styles and head patterns to ones I feel are unique. I have a lot of new ideas and some painting techniques that I want to try. I admire Jim Pierce and Charlie Bryan's painting a lot.

"Paulownia, white pine, bass and cedar are the woods I prefer, and in that order. For the heads I like bass wood and sugar pine. I've used oil base since I started and have no intention to change from that. Making my feathering brushes is an art in itself.

"Between the decoys I have made for Jim and myself I feel I have made around twelve thousand since 1981.

"Chris Burley was the first person to collect my birds and has helped me to establish a new shop that will open at the Stepping Stone Museum in Harford County.

"My dad has taken me hunting since I was twelve years old. First it was goose hunting on the Eastern Shore. We have both hunted in Wyoming and have brought back elk. In 1989 we plan to body-boot on the flats with a goose rig I am making. I enjoy the goose hunting more than any other type of hunting.

"I remember body-booting with Steve Lay and Derrick Remmix on the flats. It was Christmas Eve day in 1984. Steve had dropped us off in the boots and the wind was picking up. The waves started rolling in, hitting us in the chest and the temperature was around ten degrees. The water would freeze on our guns and suits as soon as it hit them. My hands had gotten wet and my gloves had frozen solid. We had one dart of geese come into the decoys but could not shoot because our guns were frozen tight. We could not signal Steve by shooting so we waved our guns in the air. After about an hour Steve picked us up. Derrick had to help me take off my gloves. He wrapped my hands in his coat. When they started to thaw out the pain was severe. Now when I body-boot I make sure I keep my hands dry at all times. It's easy to be careless out there, and when you are you pay for it."

Daniel Carson holding Canvasback drake with half-size Canada Goose in foreground.

Bottom left clockwise: half-size wooden sinkbox Canvasback hen, half-size Pintail drake, half-size Ruddy Duck hen, Full-size Canvasback drake sleeper, half-size Ruddy Duck drake, half-size Pintail hen, half-size wooden sinkbox Canvasback drake were made by Danny Carson.

John H. Clark painting half-size Whistling (Tundra) Swan.

Left front clockwise: full-size Green-winged Teal hen, full-size Canvasback drake, half-size Whistling (Tundra) Swan, full-size Canvasback hen, full-size Green-winged Teal drake made by John Clark.

John H. Clark

"I was born December 21, 1949. I work as a shop foreman for the Maryland National Guard.

"I began making decoys in 1981. I was hanging around with Pat Vincenti at that time. We hunted waterfowl on the flats in the boots. I seemed to be up at his house a lot just spending time together. I guess it just got into my blood.

"Ninety percent of the birds I make have ornamental heads on them. Birds that I know are going to thrown in the water I do put cheeks in them. I have always tried to make my birds different in their looks than anyone else. My birds are gunning style birds but with ornamental heads. This is what the collectors buy. Gunning style means there is a weight, ring and staple on the bottom of the decoy.

"I would have to guess that I have made between fifteen hundred to two thousand birds. That would include full-size and half-size.

"Like most of the other carvers I use oil paints, white pine and bass wood. I am in the process of getting a decoy machine. Right now I still turn them up at Butch Wagoner's. My half-size are flat bottom, along with my Swans.

My wife helps me quite a bit. She sands, putties and primes them. My youngest son, John, Jr. seems to be taking to the decoys. He doesn't help out, but he makes what he likes.

"Hunting is something I have done since I was about six years old. I have never bushwhacked, but I have done my share of body-booting on the flats. The only reason I have field gunned for geese is because I wasn't comfortable taking my son Steven out in the boots. I gunned out of a rig called the *Wild Turkey.* There was John Simpers, Butch Wagoner, Pat Vincenti, Glen Egans, Bruce Steelman and Alvin Steelman. I won't elaborate on any hunting stories or about what went on, but I will say we had some awful good days out on those flats.

"Decoy making is a funny business. But it is the best business to be in. People that you thought would never help you with a problem will be more then willing to help if you ask. They are all that way. They are a special breed of people. There is only one time they are hard to get information out of. That is when you try to find out where they get their wood. They don't want to tell you none of that."

Canada Goose decoy sits on gunnel as Mr. Clark suits up to body-boot on the "Flats." Mickey McMullen made goose decoy out of styrofoam glued to a wood flat bottom. After attaching head the body was covered with epoxy and rolled in wood chips. After drying it was painted flat black.

Robert "Bob" Coleman holding cork Black Duck.

Part of decoy weight collection belonging to Bob Coleman.

Robert "Bob" Coleman

"I was born June 8, 1921 near Crumpton in Queen Ann County, Maryland. I graduated from high school and started working. I have worked as a salesman, a parts man for a dealer, a book keeper, and, at the last, a substitute mail driver.

"I started making decoys in 1959. Sugar pine, bass and jelutong are my favorite woods. I make the decoy to look as much like the real bird as possible. Oil base paints are all I use. I try to get the softness and blending when I paint. I have learned that from Charlie Joiner, Lem Ward and Elmer Crowell.

"One time a man said he would give me two Canvasbacks for each Mallard that I would make him. I made him a dozen Mallards and got twenty-four Canvasback decoys. After that I started to make decoys for myself. Almost all of the decoys I have made have been flat bottom birds.

"I guess I have made over five hundred gunning birds. One time I took a green wing teal down for Lem Ward to see. Lem said 'the colors are the same as on a pintail.' He painted a pintail the colors of a green wing just to show me what he was talking about, then wiped it off with a rag. He said, 'I am glad to see that you are not satisfied with your work, that is the only way you will ever improve. If you think you are the best in the beginning, you will never get any better.'

"No doubt about it, I believe that Charlie Joiner is the best decoy maker on the bay today. He has learned from the best there was and came up with his own unique style. Any one who knows decoys can identify a Joiner right away. They have been highly sought after for years. Since he was honored at Havre de Grace their value has really gone up. Speed has a great sense of humor with all those little country sayings of his. He can make you laugh at the smallest things.

"I started hunting in the sixties. One day Mr. Jack McKinney and Mr. Voschell from up the road came down with a hundred and fifty decoys that Mr. John McKinney had made. He was a nephew of Henry Lochard. We put out all of those decoys plus my own spread. It made the biggest rig out there that day. I couldn't see that it made any difference. When the ducks are flying you will do pretty good anyway.

"We got real good shooting on the Chester River when the Flats froze up. There were many of good days in the 1960s. The action would be fast and furious with Canvasbacks. Then the Blackheads would start buzzing our rig. My Chesapeake would work her heart out. I could watch her eyes and tell when something was coming that we could shoot at. She ignored Sea Gulls and Crows, but when it was ducks or geese her eyes would get brighter and brighter. Norris Pratt said, 'If I had never fired my gun I would have had a good day just watching "Missy" work.'"

Flat bottom cork Black Duck with Charles "Speed" Joiner's shotgun in the rear. When Speed Joiner quit hunting he gave his favorite shotgun to Bob.

Captain William "Bill" Collins

"I was born May 15, 1949 and was raised in Perryville, Maryland. After I graduated from Perryville High, then I went to Baltimore Institute for Computer Programing, but did not care for it too much. On June 10, 1969 I came across the river (Susquehanna) and started working for Mr. R. Madison Mitchell. When you worked for Mr. Mitchell you made decoys also. It was then I went on to school in New York City at Funeral Director's College. After twelve months I received my license for Funeral Director and Embalmer, and I still hold my license for both."

"My first experience in making decoys was when I was about fifteen years old; my brother and I made some decoys to gun over on the flats. After I was done working for Mr. Mitchell, I would hang around Mr. Ed Sampson's shop a couple nights a week. That is where I learned the basics of head whittling. Mr. Mitchell taught me the finer points of decoy making.

"The styles of birds I've made has been influenced by Mr. Mitchell the most. The collection of flat bottom gunning birds I made for the 1989 Havre de Grace Decoy Festival showed the influence of Mitchell, Ward Brothers, and Charlie Joiner. Charlie Joiner has been helpful to me. I was very fortunate in that respect. He has always been very open with his knowledge. I have found it to be that way with all true decoy makers. You take what you like from one person's style and include it into your own decoy. After several hundred years of decoy making, how much are you going to be able to change a decoy? It's all been done; you're just repeating what has been done before."

"I don't expect to see any of my flat bottom decoys being gunned over because of the price. I may make a few for myself to gun over some day."

"Bass wood, sugar pine, and white cedar are my favorite woods for decoys. The white cedar I like best for the flat style gunning decoy I'm making now. I will still be making round bottom decoys from time to time because it's hard to break away completely from what you've been doing in the past."

Captain William "Bill" Collins feathers a Black Duck while Canvasback drake sits in the foreground. Captain Collins was selected as Honorary Chairman for the Havre de Grace Decoy Festival in 1989. Complete collection of Bill's decoys were sold at auction.

Top, flat bottom Canvasback hen. Bottom, flat bottom Canvasback drake by Captain Collins.

Top, flat bottom Mallard hen. Bottom, flat bottom Mallard drake by Bill Collins.

Top view of Mallard hen shows Captain Collins's feather detail.

"When it comes to the flat bottom decoys the paints I prefer are tube oils and the basic Japan colors with the various driers. The round bottom birds I paint with your regular oils out of the can, with Japan colors and driers."

"The flat bottom decoys are cut on a band saw while the round bottom decoys are turned out on a machine similar to a lathe. The machine I had came from Mr. Bob McGaw and sold to Mr. Mitchell who then sold it to me in 1980 or 1981. I have since sold it to the Havre de Grace Decoy Museum. Three generations of decoy makers used that machine that has turned out countless numbers of decoys. As far as I'm concerned it is still the best machine in Harford County today. The amount of decoys I have made over the years on that machine would have to be a guess, because I really do not know."

"The two greatest men in my life have been my father and Mr. Mitchell. Without these two men I would not be where I am in decoy making today. You hear people say 'I did this' and 'I did that,' well I didn't do everything. I had my father and Mr. Mitchell behind me. I'll tell you one thing, when you have people like that behind you it's hard to go wrong. My dad had his own little corner of the shop with a "Do Not Disturb" sign. He would help me from time to time by making lamp bases and by bending the brass for the lamps. He made a half size goose scooter for Mr. Mitchell and himself, also he made several carver benches."

"I employed my nephew, Michael Collins, in the shop for several years. He can make an excellent decoy. He does not make them now because he chose another line of work. He has the knowledge to make decoys himself or to work for someone else if he wishes some day. The head is the hardest step in decoy making, and Michael is an excellent head maker."

"Pat Vincenti, who is a bit younger than I am, has been very influential to me the last few years. We have both benefited from our relationship, and I believe we have both improved greatly in our decoy making. Pat, I believe, makes probably one of the best working decoys in this area today.

Mr. Mitchell always told me, 'If you finish a decoy today look it over and try to improve on it the next time.' He said if you improve to a point where you think the decoys you're making are good enough, you're done for. That's as good as you'll ever get. There will be no more natural progression to get better."

"Senators and congressman have purchased my decoys. I made a pair of decoys for Governor Schaefer. The best compliment I ever had was a comment from Willie Parker, Federal Agent in charge of the Delmarva Peninsula. (It didn't come directly to me, but I helped make some of the decoys). He made the statement that Madison Mitchell made the best Canvasbacks he had ever seen in his life. He said he was patrolling on the Potomac one day and spotted some

Top, flat bottom American Widgeon (Baldpate) drake. Bottom, flat bottom American Widgeon (Baldpate) hen by Captain Collins.

Flat bottom Brant by Bill Collins.

Canvasbacks as he was coming around a point in a skiff. He watched them for while and wanted to make a count of them. Only as he moved closer did he realize they were decoys instead of live ducks. He rowed on in to the blind and found out they were all Mitchell decoys. You've got to stop and think about that, here is a man who has been around waterfowl all his life and was ready to count a bunch of decoys in the end of year survey."

"When I first started with Mr. Mitchell, 75% of the decoys were sold to people who were gunning over them. They sold for about $8.50 for Canvasbacks and $9.00 for Mallards each."

"I was ten or twelve years old when my dad took my brother and I squirrel hunting. My brother taught me about waterfowl hunting. I had the opportunity to go bushwhacking one time in my life. I killed one Canvasback which was the limit then. One of my most memorable hunts was down on the eastern shore in Ingleside. There were three guides and we had fifteen gunners that morning in three parties. It was an unusual day, we could have killed two hundred Snow geese that day; they just kept coming in. We ended up with 67 snows, 2 blues and 3 Canada geese, all legal limits. We were 1 snow and 2 blues short of the limit at that time.

I quit guiding several years ago because of the shortage of game. I now guide fishing parties for Captain Buddy Harris out of Tilghman Island, from spring till fall. The decoys I make in the winter months."

Top, flat bottom Goldeneye hen. Bottom, flat bottom Goldeneye drake by Captain Collins.

Flat bottom Canada Goose by Bill Collins.

Top, flat bottom Green-winged Teal hen. Bottom, flat bottom Green-winged Teal drake by Captain Collins.

Top, flat bottom Blackhead hen. Bottom, flat bottom Blackhead drake by Captain Collins.

Top, flat bottom Pintail drake. Bottom, flat bottom Pintail hen by Captain Collins.

Top, flat bottom Bufflehead hen. Bottom, flat bottom Bufflehead drake by Captain Collins.

Flat bottom Black Duck by Captain Collins.

Captain Bill Collins sets out flat bottom cork Wood Ducks at dawn on Furnace Creek. Chesapeake Bay Retriever sits along side as Bill poles boat.

Flat bottom cork Wood Ducks made by Madison Mitchell and Bill Collins are ready to be put over board for first time. Only fourteen cork Wood Ducks were made.

Joseph Coudon
Born: 1860 lived in Aiken, Cecil County, Maryland
Died: 1947

Mallard V-boards made by Joseph Coudon.

Blackhead V-boards in original shipping box made by Mr. Coudon.

Relief carving of flying hen and drake Canvasback by Mr. Coudon.

Black Duck V-boards made by Mr. Coudon.

Canvasback drake wooden sinkbox decoy made by Joseph Coudon.

Top, Canvasback drake. Bottom, Canvasback hen by Mr. Coudon.

Canada Goose V-boards made by Mr. Coudon.

Relief carving of Whistling (Tundra) Swan.

Relief carving of Wood Duck family made by Mr. Coudon.

Woodcock and Quail carvings made by Mr. Coudon.

James "Jim" Alexander Currier
Born: 1886 lived in Havre De Grace, Harford County, Maryland
Died: 1971

Top, Canvasback drake. Bottom, Canvasback hen made by James "Jim" Alexander Currier.

Mallard drake made by Mr. Currier.

Green-winged Teal drake by Jim Currier.

Miniature decoys made by Mr. Currier. Top left clockwise: miniature Canvasback drake, miniature Redhead drake, miniature Redhead hen, miniature Canvasback hen.

Henry Davis
Born: 1875 lived in Perryville, Cecil County, Maryland
Died: 1956

Canvasback hen by Henry Davis.

Edward Duffy
Born: 1895 lived in Chesapeake City, Cecil County, Maryland
Died: 1983

Over-size Canvasback silhouette decoy made by Edward Duffy.

Bottom view of over-size Canvasback silhouette decoy made by Edward Duffy.

Captain Ben Dye
Born: 1821 lived in Stump's Point, Cecil County, Maryland
Died: 1896

Redhead drake by Captain Ben Dye.

Joseph Dye
Born: 1870 lived in Havre de Grace, Harford County, Maryland
Died: 1931

Blackhead drake made by Joseph "Joe" Dye.

George Alfred Edwards, Jr.

"I was born June 27, 1907. Bengies, Maryland has always been my home. I had eight grades of schooling at Piney Grove, then became a boat builder like my father.

"Through the years from 1915 to 1955 my father and I built fifty-five boats that ranged in length from twenty-five feet to forty-two feet. Forty were work boats for fishing and crabbing. Fifteen were built as Sport Fishermen between 1955 to 1967. We also built countless rowboats.

"My father taught me how to make decoys in 1924, when I was seventeen years old. We never had anyone to show us how to make decoys so we just did the best we could. You would find decoys floating in the river and on the shore were they broke loose from someone's rig. We would pick them up to use and if we liked the looks of it we would try to make decoys similar to it.

"The first decoys were Redhead duck V-Boards. We used cedar, white pine and four inch thick cork for the bodies. All the decoys were painted with flat boat paint. We molded our weights and made our rings for the bottoms.

"Every decoy we made was handmade. We never had a decoy machine. A band saw, spoke shave, knife and sander were the only tools we had.

"Between my dad and myself we made a thousand or more decoys in our time. Today I could not tell you where you could find one though. We lost the last of our own rig in a garage fire years ago in the forties. Local gunners and friends were our customers mainly. We did give some away as gifts. I remember sending some to North Carolina, Vermont, and Texas. All I have left is a Canvasback head made out of mahogany. It was the last thing I made. [It was given to the author to place in the Havre de Grace Museum]

"My father took me hunting when I was a boy. He had three blinds off Carrols Island. Salt Peter Creek and Spry's Island were great places to hunt ducks back then. Spry's Island was washed away in 1942 or 1943. We also hunted geese on the Eastern Shore in Church Creek and East Neck Island. Redheads, Blue Bills, and Baldpates were the ducks we shot the most in this area.

"We took duck hunting parties for a while. Over the years we owned three Chesapeake water dogs. Eleanor, Lazy Bones, and Bobby Johnson were their names. I can't reflect on any one hunt in particular, I just remember hunting ducks when there was no limit. We lived up to the law. We baited when it was legal and we didn't night gun." Mr. Edwards passed away in 1989.

George Alfred Edwards Jr. is holding the last piece he made, a mahogany Canvasback head. Behind Mr. Edwards lies one of the historic "Edwards" yachts.

Full-size decorative Whistling (Tundra) Swan. The only one Mr. Edwards made.

American Coot V-boards made by George Alfred Edwards Jr.

American Widgeon (baldpate) V-boards made by Mr. Edwards.

Full-size Canada Goose decoy made of World War Two Balsa wood life raft. Decoy made by George Edwards.

Full-size Canvasback drake made by Mr. Edwards.

Standley Evans
Born: 1887 lived in Elkton, Cecil County, Maryland
Died: unknown

Blackhead hen by Standley Evans.

Blackhead drake by Mr. Evans.

Columbus "Lum" Fletcher
Born: 1867 lived in Swan Creek, Harford County, Maryland
Died: 1942

Canvasback drake by Columbus "Lum" Fletcher.

Howard "Duck" Israel Foreaker

"It was July 9, 1933 when I was born in a farm house in North East, Maryland. North East is where I went to school. I stayed till the tenth grade. I've worked as a union carpenter since I started working.

"The gunning boats I make are one-fifth scale. I make four styles of boats. The bushwhack boat, rail bird boat, night gunning skiff and the big gun skiff. I have made over one hundred since I made the first one. It was a bushwhack boat that was made for the first North East Waterfowl Show. I have made more bushwhack boats than the others. I make pump shot guns, anchors, oars, sculling oar, shot gun shells and shell box to go inside the boat. The boat measures forty-three inches long by twelve inches wide. My wife sews the white curtains for the front of the boat.

"White pine is the only wood I make them from. They are put together with one half inch, no. 20 finishing nails and glue. White Rustoleum paint is the only paint I use. I'll start out with a four quarter or five quarter board and rip it to three sixteenths. The tools I use to make the boats are the table saw, band saw, planner and a block plane. It takes me about fifteen hours to make a bushwhack boat.

The boat floats real nice. We put one over one time and laid a good size Rock Fish in it. It hung over both ends of the boat. Then we took a picture of it. They're all gone now, but I think Jimmy Pierce has one hanging up in his shop. I have given more of those boats away then I ever sold.

"When I was a kid I made some decoys to gun over. I made full-bodied geese and Canvasbacks. I never made very many, only enough to gun over. It was only lately that I began to make decoys to sell. I machine turn the bodies on a machine I made myself. The patterns I use are the Lochard's. I guess I favor them the most since I grew up with that heritage. I am related to the Lochards through my mother. I am making Redheads and Canvasbacks. You will notice that I don't paint wings on the back. That's the way the Lochards made them. After the sinkbox was outlawed they started putting wing feathers on them. They though it would hold the ducks in there longer.

"I gunned with Harry and Wilson Reynolds. They are grand-children of George Lochard. We did most of our gunning on the Flats. Ducks were our main thing. We would gun Canvasbacks out of the bushwhack rig and Blackheads in the shore blinds. We baited everything. You can't beat corn for baiting. It works great. Every one baited, they just don't admit it. You start baiting about three weeks before the gunning season. Those diving ducks will find it up to twenty feet deep. While we were running the boat real slow, we would pour about twenty bushel over the back and let the motor scatter it. Down in Carrot Cove, they used to have corn in there a foot deep. You could see it from an airplane. That's how the game warden would catch you most of the time. I was never caught but, I came close. The most Canvasbacks I remember killing was about fifty in one day. The geese love corn too. The game wardens got pretty slick towards the last. I have got a lot of respect for Norman Biggs and Alfred Grew. Biggs was state and Grew was a federal game warden. They would give you a break."

Howard "Duck" Israel Foreaker holds pair of Canvasbacks he made in 1989.

Mr. Foreaker holds Puntgun Skiff with Bushwhack boat in foreground.

Close-up shows detail on Bushwhack boat and contents. Everything is handmade to one fifth scale. Winchester model 12 shotguns are also made of wood Mr. Foreaker.

James "Jimmy" Frey completes paint on Mallard drake with finished Pintail in background.

James "Jimmy" Frey

"I was born January 28, 1948 in Havre de Grace, Maryland and raised on the Bush River on the Otter Point Dairy Farm. After getting my high school diploma and a diploma from the Vocational Technical Center in Building Trades, I became an equipment operator for construction equipment.

"I started making decoys because it was our way of life. Being raised on the Bush River I knew a lot of the old market gunners. Buck Leight was one of them. He had the big pound gun. In *Outlaw Gunner* they do have his name mentioned.

"All my relatives gunned. It goes as far back as I can remember. When I was small it was my job to row the boat. When the old timers were still alive, if they wanted you to go in a certain area you had better be able to put that boat there or you were liable to get a good sized fist upside the head. They would want to know what the hell was the matter with me, was I crazy or just plain simple. There was a lot of times I would have to stand up and pull just as hard as I could to get that big boat in there. The boat was a 20 footer. Kids were raised a little tougher in those days. Like I said all my relatives were gunners. A lot of them gunned for market, and then, when that was outlawed, they still gunned.

"I made my first decoy thirty years ago. I made it off of a piece of my fathers bar. What happened was one of the old panels came off of the side. They were all one inch stock. What I did was took an old hand saw, sawed it off and took common nails, beaded an outline of a duck and put a head on it. It floated. To hold it in your hands it didn't look very good, but out in the water it wasn't too bad.

"My grandfather made some decoys. I still have his decoy vise. I guess I will stop making decoys when I can't do it any more.

Full size hand-chopped decoys by Jimmy Frey are left front clockwise: Mallard hen, Canvasback drake, Whistling (Tundra) Swan, Canvasback hen, Mallard drake.

"I would have to say Howard and Buddy Gunther, my uncles, had a small influence on my style of decoy making. But my biggest influence was Paul Gibson. Around 1978 I was making a few decoys with my Uncle Buddy. One day he asked me how I was doing and I told him not so good. He looked at then and said, 'Hell, son, I can't teach you anything. Why don't you go see Paul Gibson?' I told him I didn't know Mr. Gibson. Come to find out Paul had been on our farm dozens of times but I just didn't know who he was.

I went to Paul and told him who I was. He never said a word. Just sat there looking at me kind of funny. I told him Buddy Gunther sent me to see if he could help me with my decoy making. Paul asked me how I knew Buddy and when I told him he was my uncle he kind of laughed and said, 'Let me see what you've got.' I showed him and he said, 'Well, what's wrong with it?' In other words he made you pick it apart yourself. Paul was painting that day I first met him. He asked me what I was doing the next weekend. When I told him I didn't know he asked me if I wanted to learn how to make ducks. Of course I jumped at the chance. I never asked him for a job, though. He also influenced my painting style, very much so. I worked for Paul for a little over five years before he passed away.

"All I ever use is oil base paint. The wood I use on the bodies is white pine and I try to use white pine heads. I still carve all my decoys by hand. None of them are machine made. If I had to guess I would say I have probably made a couple thousand decoys.

"My style of decoys have changed from when I first started. For one thing the head styles are different. They still look similar to Paul's, but some way or other they are different. I've changed the bill thickness and the lengths. My bodies are all heavy compared to some people's. But that goes back to the days when we wanted a heavy decoy to withstand the gunning.

"As for my customers, they would be any body who wants them. I would imagine most of them are gunners.

"Without a doubt my favorite species of duck is the Canvasback when it comes for looks and respect. I enjoyed eating them too. To me eating a Canvasback compared to any other duck is like comparing a T-bone to a hamburger. There is no comparison.

"I can recall a couple of memorable hunts. One time was back in 1958 on Dr. Davis's farm. I was hunting with my father and my uncle. We killed five feed bags full of Canvasbacks in two passes. A feed bag holds approximately twenty birds. Another time was in 1976. I was hunting with my brother-in-law, Gene, on the Eastern Shore. We crawled up to a pond and jumped the geese that were on the water. Gene's gun jammed, so he only killed one. I killed eighteen with three shots. I was glad the other guys on our farm were there that day because they had to cover for me.

"When my Uncle Howard passed away I was completely devastated. He meant an awful lot to me. He was basically the reason I'm into decoy making today. Well, he passed away on a Friday. Every Saturday I went to Paul's shop to work. If I wasn't there by 10:00 in the morning Paul would call me. I got to thinking about what my uncle would want me to do. He always liked to see me making decoys. So I decided that was what I would do. I hadn't told Paul my uncle had passed away, but my wife called him after I left the house to inform him I was feeling bad. When I got there Paul never said a word to me about it. I started working around the shop, then, all at once it hit me again about the loss of my uncle. Paul came to me and put those big hands of his on my shoulders and said, 'You know there's a lot of things in this world that we hate to do. But we have got to do them. There comes a time when we have to bury our dead. Every day you think about him and every day that you talk about him it will get a little easier.' Paul was basically right about that. Paul meant a lot to me. He was like a grandfather to me. I will never forget him and how he tried to comfort me when I needed it the most. I sure miss him."

Mr. Frey is shown working with Paul Gibson in Paul's shop.

Paul Gibson is painting Baldpate drake. Mallard drake, Canvasback drake, Baldpate drake and unfinished Canvasback sit on the paint table.

Paul Gibson (As told by Mary E. Gibson)

"Paul was born August 1, 1902 in Havre de Grace, Maryland.

"Paul went as far as the eighth grade. He would have gone further in school but his father died and he had to go to work to help out at home.

"Paul worked for my uncle for twenty-four years in the grocery store. Then after that he worked at Edgewood as a fireman for twenty-five years. He was a chief for a right good while, but he liked to work every other day so that he could be in his shop making decoys. The fire department let him do that and he was real happy about that. He was very strict with the men down there, but they all seemed to like him. He had charge of four fire houses and about fifty men. I still hear from them once in a while.

"Paul made his first decoy when he was 13 years old. I still have it. I believe it is a Canvasback. Of course, it is pretty rough looking. It needs fixing up. I bought one of those glass cones and I have it in that. I told my nephew I would give it to him. If anything happens to my nephew it goes to the museum.

"Paul was self-taught as far as decoy making goes. He never worked for anybody. He never learned from anyone.

"He started making decoys because he loved to work with his hands. He loved to do carpentry work and he loved to hunt. He built a couple of houses, two cruisers and I don't know how many row boats. He used to have a small shop not too far from here, that was in the 1940s. He was making decoys then to sell for $1.50 a pair.

"When Paul first started he made his decoys by hand. All hand-chopped. I will say this, of all the decoys that Paul has ever made, I don't think he ever had any brought back to him. Only to be repaired after they had been used a lot. His paint job and everything was perfect."

Mr. Gibson assembles the last Whistling (Tundra) Swan he made.

Mr. Gibson was selected as Honorary Chairman at the Havre de Grace Decoy Festival in 1983. Paul and his wife Mary are standing next to the full-size decoy collection that was sold at auction.

"Paul made his last decoys about 1983. He was honored in May of that year and he made a few more after that until he went into the hospital that November. Paul passed away January 24, 1985.

"Paul's style was his own. The painting and everything. The patterns are still here.

"The woods that he used were cedar and pine. For the heads it was pine. The paints were oil. The best that you could get.

"When Paul first started he hand-chopped his decoys. He bought his first machine from Madison Mitchell around 1945. From that time on they were machine made.

"I wouldn't want to even try to guess as to how many decoys Paul made in his life time. If I said 5,000 it wouldn't be enough and if I said 100,000 it might be too much.

"We had no children, so sometimes I would help him out with the wood. Saw it out on the band saw. But I never did any decoy work. That was strictly his shop and he wanted to do it. When he first opened his big shop his niece's husband helped out some. Then about eight or nine years before Paul died George Hendricks came to work for him. Jimmy Frey came about the same time too, but that was only on weekends.

"Over the years, as time passed, he never really changed his style. He only made a working decoy.

"The majority of Paul's customers were hunters. Then toward the last few years people started collecting them for decorative purposes. I recall our doctor in Baltimore had a place on Gibson Island and he bought some decoys for around his fireplace. Well, they had a very bad fire and all the decoys were destroyed. The doctor wanted Paul to make him some more. You know, he wanted to buy them. But Paul told him no. Paul said he knew how much he was hurt that he had lost the decoys in the fire, so Paul made them and gave them to him. That doctor never, never, forgot that.

"Paul loved to hunt. He just loved the water, too. His hunting partners were my cousin and my uncle. He used to go to Cecil County with his cousin David Gibson and Arthur Mitchell. Years ago he used to hunt in a sinkbox. He did a lot of bushwhacking, too. I think my uncle was almost like a father to Paul. Paul's father died when he was only two years old. My uncle taught Paul a lot as far as hunting went.

"He always had hunting dogs. We had Beagles. We loved those dogs. They were part of our family. We used to talk to them like they were people. Paul never owned a water dog.

"I can't recall if Paul had one hunt that stood out from the rest. If he was sitting here now I guess he could tell you. Waterfowl hunting was his favorite type of hunting. To see those ducks flying and shooting them. Oh my, he just loved that.

"Around 1965 Paul lost the sight in his right eye due to acute glaucoma. He made a gun stock to gun with. It was so successful that he made another for someone else. He was right-handed so he made the gun stock to use under his left eye shooting from a right-handed position. I only have one of Paul's guns left. I've sold all the rest of them. It wasn't any use for me to keep them. I do have a few decoys left, but the museum gets them."

Top, Canvasback drake. Bottom, Canvasback hen by Paul Gibson.

Top, Mallard drake sleeper. Bottom, Mallard hen sleeper by Mr. Gibson.

Top, American Widgeon (Baldpate) drake. Bottom, American Widgeon (Baldpate) hen by Mr. Gibson.

Black Duck made by Mr. Gibson.

Top, Canvasback hen sleeper. Bottom, Canvasback hen sleeper by Paul Gibson.

Top, Blackhead hen. Bottom, Blackhead drake by Mr. Gibson.

Canada Goose sleeper by Mr. Gibson.

Top, American Goldeneye hen. Bottom, American Goldeneye drake by Mr. Gibson.

Top, Redhead hen. Bottom, Redhead drake by Mr. Gibson.

Top, Bufflehead drake. Bottom, Bufflehead hen by Mr. Gibson.

Top, Green-winged Teal drake. Bottom, Green-winged Teal hen by Mr. Gibson.

Top, Blue-winged Teal hen. Bottom, Blue-winged Teal drake by Mr.Gibson.

Top, Pintail hen. Bottom, Pintail drake by Mr. Gibson.

Shotgun stock Paul Gibson made for himself. Paul was right handed and blind in his right eye. Stock was made so he could shoot with his left eye.

Paul Gibson with last Canada geese he made.

Captain John "Johnny" Glen
Born: 1876 lived in Rock Hall, Kent County, Maryland
Died: 1954

Pintail drake made by Captain John "Johnny" Glen.

Horace D. Graham
Born: 1893 lived in Charlestown, Cecil County, Maryland
Died: 1981

Top, Mallard hen. Bottom, Mallard drake made by Horace Graham.

Snow Goose by Horace Graham.

John B. Graham
Born: 1822 lived in Charlestown, Cecil County, Maryland
Died: 1912

Canvasback drake by John B. Graham.

Canvasback hen by Mr. Graham.

Canvasback drake ice decoy by Mr. Graham.

Severn Wallis Hall

"I was born on February 13, 1909 in North East, Maryland. I attended high school and studied Electrical Engineering at Drexel Institute in Philadelphia. I worked as a private yacht captain for the Dilks family of Philadelphia. I also worked with Captain Bilsbough for Felix DuPont, Sr., and sailed from New Castle, Delaware to the West Indies on their 75 foot sports sword fishing boat the "Buckruo."

"Decoy making started with me as a hobby, later it became my livelihood. I first started painting decoys at age 12 or 13 and continued through high school. I also painted for William Heverin of Charlestown, Maryland. I received five cents each for drake Canvasback and ten cents each for hen Canvasback and furnished the paint. Jake Mowery of Lancaster, Pennsylvania and Mr. Heverin influenced my painting style. As far as the style of the body, I had a desire to develop a good rough water decoy. I noticed that most decoys would not function above twenty-five mile-per-hour winds. I developed various patterns from choice specimens of various ducks.

"My father had charge of Mr. Melrath's sinkbox rig. They had about seven hundred decoys in that rig. Pop had hired Mr. Heverin to come over and repaint those decoys and told him that my brother Dick and I would help him. Well my brother Dick was always carrying on foolishly. And Mr. Heverin's nickname was "Snake." He had always been afraid of snakes of all kinds. We would see lots of Blacksnakes around the river and around those swamps. Well, that brother of mine went out into the swamp behind of the boat house and killed a blacksnake about three feet long. Mr. Heverin and I were at the table painting. I used to put the white on the backs and bodies of the Canvasback decoys and hand them to Mr. Heverin. He would put the black paint on the breast and tail. He would finish the head off and set the decoy up in the rack to dry.

"Well, Mr. Heverin and I were about half finished with another decoy when my brother Dick came in with the snake on a stick. He dropped it in the middle of the paint table. Paint cans looked like they exploded. Mr. Heverin had kicked the table while trying to get away. I did not care for snakes either so I went the other way. My brother stood there laughing. I can still hear Mr. Heverin cussing my brother.

"Eastern white pine from old bridges and barns was the main wood source I had. I also made decoys from refrigeration cork. As for paints, I used house paints, lead and oils. Later I used synthetic paints. All the decoys I made were handmade without the use of a machine. I used a band saw, drum sander, various hand tools, and spoke shaves.

"I have made several hundred decoys. I have repaired and repainted thousands of decoys for hunters until I quit in 1965. I was getting thirty-five cents a decoy plus paint when I quit. John Schaeffer of Chesapeake City, Maryland was my most famous customer. He kept me busy with repairs and repainting his personal decoys.

"I loved the Canvasback to eat. I called them the Royal Stoggie. For years I hunted with Earl Melrath, Andrew Reynolds and Captain Frank Jackson. I gunned with Jackson for two years before I realized that he only had one eye. He was an expert and deadly shot.

"Bushwhacking on the flats was my favorite way of gunning. Jake Mowery and I were bushwhacking one day in 1946 for Canvasbacks. We were doing well when a storm blew in. The forty foot Skipjack being used for the mother ship was forced to drag anchor. We boarded the mother boat before taking up decoys because it was drifting away fast. It was brought under control after we played out seventy five more foot of anchor line. The wind was blowing so hard the air was filled with dust and feathers. Decoys were finally recovered with the use of our bushwhack boat and a five horse power Johnson outboard motor and oars. Harbor was finally gained under jib with the mainsail furled, and the wind was singing "The Song of the Rose Tree."

Flat bottom cork with wooden keel Canvas-back drake made by Severin Hall.

American Coot (Crowbill) by Mr. Hall.

Tom Harman

"I was born April 5, 1954 in Havre de Grace, Maryland. I lived most of my life in Aberdeen, Maryland.

"I have a Bachelor of Science Degree in Engineering, and am an engineer at Aberdeen Proving Grounds.

"I started making decoys in 1971 at Capt'n Harry Jobes shop. I also worked a little bit for Charlie Bryan. I first met Mr. Bryan when I was little. My dad had a lathe and Mr. Bryan used to come up and turn bodies on it.

"As a kid I used to hunt on the Proving Grounds and we didn't have any Black Duck decoys so I started making some. I guess the reason I began making decoys was my association with hunting.

"My dad used to make his own decoys also. There again he was like every one else at the time. He couldn't afford to buy them and there was plenty of wood around and everybody made their own to hunt with. He and George Hendricks made Canvasbacks together. This was around the earlyto mid-fifties. That was long before George got in with Paul Gibson. When Canvasback started to disappear my dad and George quit making decoys. Then my dad's shop burned down and they lost the machine. Mr. Bryan's machine is built on a duplication of my father's.

"I used to work in Mr. Mitchell's shop after I left Jobes. Then, when Mr. Mitchell quit, I went to work for Jimmy Pierce. All along I was helping Charlie Bryan maybe a weekend or so, here and there. I like the way Charlie Joiner paints, so I have tried to pick up something from everybody I have associated with. I guess you could say they have all influenced my style. I like the way Mr. Bryan puts a decoy together and, like I said, I like the way Charlie Joiner paints them. I learned a lot about working with poles and getting the blocks cut out from Mr. Mitchell. I certainly had a good crew to work with. I learned a lot from all of them.

Robert T. Harman finishes painting pigeon decoy. Blackhead drake in background with Blackhead hen in foreground.

Left clockwise: white pigeon decoy, full-size Mallard hen, grey pigeon decoy, full-size Mallard drake by Mr. Harman.

Left, Miniature Whistling Swan. Right, miniature whistling Swan sleeper. Swans measure 2½ inches long and are one piece by Mr. Harman.

"I prefer to use white pine and bass wood for my decoys and I use oil base paints for painting.

"I don't have a machine of my own so Mr. Bryan said I could have his because I have more room for it at my place. It will still be his machine. He is only giving it up in the sense that it won't be in his garage.

"I am still fairly new at decoy making so I guess I have only made about four hundred so far. All ducks and pigeons. No geese. My wife helps me paint, prime and putty. She likes doing it.

"I really haven't gotten into decoy making enough to employ anybody. I have shown a few people how to make decoys. Not for money or any official classes.

"My different changes in carving I guess would be that I just tried to improve techniques to improve the looks of the bird. I've changed more toward Charlie Joiner's painting style and Mr. Bryan's Mallard. I would like to paint the fancier ones. I'm going to have to paint some gunning decoys because not everybody can afford the fancy stuff.

"I started waterfowl hunting when I was ten years old. I would go with my dad and Mr. Bryan at the Proving Grounds. Mr. Bryan took me to the shore a couple of times. When we went to the shore we went goose hunting and then in the middle of the day we would Quail hunt. On the Proving Grounds it was primarily Quail, Black Ducks and Mallards in the marsh. When I started hunting, Canvasbacks were pretty much done.

"My favorite species of duck to hunt is the Mallard. I still hunt a little bit today.

"I owned a bird dog. I used to take the bird dog with me and if I would knock something down in the marsh I would take the dog across in the boat. There were several times at the Proving Grounds that we limited out in ducks early in the morning.

"Each place I worked I did something a little different. When I was over at Harry Jobes I was primarily band sawing blocks and sanding. That's where I learned to sand with a belt sander. He would put a bushel of heads there and say 'Sand them.' Then you would get another bushel to sand. Just continuously sanding heads and bodies. Then I went to Mr. Mitchell's and worked out on the lot because I was the new man. Bobby Jobes and Dave Walker were working there at the time, along with Steve Lay. So I worked out on the lot and in the band saw garage when Bill wasn't band sawing. By that I mean chain sawing, splitting and blocking out. The hard part of it. From that, at least I know how to lay out a block, which is probably most important because if you don't learn that at the right place you're going to be in trouble the whole way through.

"From there I went to Jimmy Pierce's and did breasting, tailing, and running a lathe. I never did any painting with any of them that I can think of except maybe a little bit of it with Mr. Bryan. He would have me sitting across the table painting silhouette geese.

"They were all great teachers as far as I'm concerned. They answer any questions I might have and most of them would give you anything they could afford to give you. I've been pretty fortunate to have known and worked with these men."

Chris Hawkins

"I was born August 14, 1966. I've lived in Havre De Grace all my life and graduated from Havre de Grace High School.

"I work as an estimator for my father's construction company, Har-Ce Construction, Inc. In Havre de Grace.

"When I was in high school I took wood shop as a class. I met Charlie Jobes there. We would carve decoys instead of working on projects. I asked him if I could take a few heads home to carve. I used a razor utility knife. The next day he looked at my work and said it looked pretty good. With his help I obtained wood and bodies to get started in decoy making. Charlie and his brother Joey have helped me a lot.

"I was about sixteen and working for my father at Aberdeen Proving Ground when I met Butch Wagoner. I started working in his shop for over a year before setting up a shop in my parents' basement. I still go to Butch's shop for pointers and advice. I owe a lot of my skill and art to Butch and his wife Anne.

"I'm working on changing my body styles. Jim Pierce and David Walker turn my bodies for me. The head wood I get from Pierce, Wagoner, and Walker. Oil base paint and Japan colors are what I use. I have a band saw and drum sander, and also use a Foredom tool in my work.

"I don't know how many decoys I have made so far. They have been mostly miniature gunning decoys. I'm making full size gunning patterns up now.

"I hunt with the family for geese and ducks. However because of my age I missed the great days of gunning on the flats."

Chris Hawkins paints miniature Mallard drake while finished Mallard hen and Baldpates are shown on paint table.

Miniature decoys by Chris Hawkins are shown. Left front clockwise: Mallard hen Goldeneye drake, Blackhead hen, Baldpate drake, Redhead hen, Black Swan, Redhead drake, Baldpate hen, Blackhead drake, Goldeneye hen and Mallard drake.

August G. Heinefield
Born: 1883 lived in Rock Hall, Kent County, Maryland
Died: 1952

American Goldeneye drake made by August G. Heinefield.

George Edwin Hendricks

"I was born May 31, 1926 in Brookville, Pennsylvania. I was in my last year of school when my parents moved to Harford County. After I finished school I went into the service. The majority of my work life was spent working at Aberdeen Proving Ground till I retired in 1982.

"I met a guy who became a good friend of mine by the name of Max Sheets at the proving grounds. It was around 1955 or '56 when we decided to make a gunning stool of Canvasbacks. We were able to get a bunch of cedar telephone poles to use for the bodies. We cut them up in blocks and took them to Madison Mitchell. We worked out a deal with him where he would turn out two bodies for us and one for himself. I then carved the heads and rigged up a sander in the basement to sand the decoys. Then I painted them using a Mitchell Canvasback my parents had given me as a gift to go by. We had two hundred decoys when we finished.

"About a year before I retired from the government I worked for Harry Jobes. When I retired I was working a half a day for Harry and a half a day for Paul Gibson. I did this for a while and finally just worked at Paul's. I had ordered some decoys from Paul several years earlier, but never got them. Paul was so backlogged he couldn't get to them. I started out by helping him work in exchange for decoys. I wanted a set of his decoys. I worked with Paul till he passed away in January of 1985.

"I have continued to work in Paul's shop, making decoys off of his patterns. I make about two hundred decoys a year and sell them for May, Paul's wife. I have made several new patterns of my own, one is a Loon and a Puffin. I paint the same style as Paul did using oil based paint. I turn the bodies on Paul's old lathe, the one he bought from Madison Mitchell years ago.

"I have always liked to hunt. I have been doing that ever since I came here. I remember one hunt with Max Sheets. We both had children and it was Christmas Morning and we had to be back early. We were gunning on the Proving Grounds. The wind was blowing toward the shore real hard. We couldn't get the boat out because the tide was out. We started throwing the decoys out off the shore but only got half of them out when the Canvasbacks started flying into them. We all shot our limit real quick and the wind blew the ducks right in to us. We picked up the ducks and decoys and were on our way home in no time.

"Paul was one of the nicest men I've ever known. We always got a long pretty good. I loved to hear him tell all the stories of the old times. He was a great story teller."

George Hendricks paints a Puffin decoy.

William "Snake" Heverin

Born: 1860 lived in Charlestown, Cecil County, Maryland
Died: 1951

Top, Black Duck. Middle, Canvasback drake. Bottom, Canvasback hen made by William "Snake" Heverin.

Howard Hicks
Born: 1909 lived in Middle River, Baltimore County, Maryland
Died: 1971

Redhead drake by Howard Hicks.

Canvasback hen by Mr. Hicks.

Canvasback drake by Mr. Hicks.

James Holly
Born: 1855 lived in Havre De Grace, Harford County, Maryland
Died: 1935

Blue-winged Teal hen made by James "Jim" Holly.

Redhead drake made by Mr. Holly.

Captain John "Daddy" Holly
Born: 1819 lived in Havre De Grace, Harford County, Maryland
Died: 1892

Canvasback hen made by Captain Holly.

Canvasback drake made by Captain John "Daddy" Holly.

Richard T. "Dick" Houlett
Born: 1829 lived in Havre De Grace, Harford County, Maryland
Died: unknown

Canvasback drake by Richard "Dick" Houlett.

George W. Jackson
Born: 1856 lived in Perryville, Cecil County, Maryland
Died: 1898

Canvasback drake made by George Jackson.

Scott Jackson
Born: 1852 lived in Charlestown, Cecil County, Maryland
Died: 1929

Canvasback hen by Scott Jackson.

Canvasback drake by Mr. Jackson.

Captain Harry Jobes painting full-size Whistling (Tundra) Swan. Captain Jobes was selected as Honorary Chairman for the Havre de Grace Decoy Festival in 1988. Complete collections of Captain Jobes decoys were sold at auction.

Captain Harry Jobes

"I was born in 1936 in Havre de Grace, Maryland. I did the whole nine yards in school.

"One of the first jobs I worked at out of school was plastering. I have operated a patrol boat for the government off Aberdeen Proving Ground for several years. For forty three years I owned and operated my own boat. I fished nets, crabbed and took fishing and gunning parties. I've also made a few duck decoys too.

"I was a kid about eight years old when I first started fooling around with decoys in old man Charles Barnard's shop on Oak Street in Havre de Grace. Decoys fascinated me then, and they still do today. You take ninety percent of the people today and show them a decoy and they'll tell you it's just a wooden decoy. They have no idea what it means to the rest of us, we know what that decoy is and what it does. Years ago you only found decoy makers around the water. Now you'll find decorative decoy carvers in a penthouse in New York City.

"I had made a decoy in old man Barnard's shop that everyone thought looked good. I entered it in an art show contest at the high school to see how it would do. It was there I met Mrs. Helen Mitchell who was displaying some of her husband's decoys. My decoys looked like a chicken had scratched over them compared to Mr. Mitchell's. Mrs. Mitchell looked at my decoy and offered me a job working in her husband's shop. I turned the job offer down and went on back to Barnard's shop. A year later old man Barnard died. It was then I went to see Mrs. Mitchell for a job. I must have been ten or twelve at that time. I knocked on the Mitchell's door and Mrs. Mitchell answered. She hired me right then, not Madison. Then she went to the shop to tell pop I was working for him.

"The jobs ranged from sweeping the floors to any of the duck making chores. You would work in the wood pile first, using the spoke shave and draw knife. Puttying and sanding came next, then priming the decoys. Mitchell never taught me how to whittle duck

Decoy pattern turns against tracing wheel in Captain Harry's decoy machine.

Wooden block is turned into decoy body in Captain Harry's decoy machine.

Captain Harry Jobes's wife, Helen, helps to make the decoys and takes care of the shipping.

Top left clockwise: full-size Cinnamon Teal drake, full-size Cinnamon Teal hen, miniature Cinnamon Teal drake, miniature Cinnamon Teal hen made by Captain Jobes.

Top left clockwise: full-size Green-winged Teal hen, full-size Green-winged Teal drake, miniature Green-winged Teal drake, miniature Green-winged Teal hen made by Captain Jobes.

Top left clockwise: full-size American Widgeon (baldpate) hen, full-size American Widgeon (baldpate) drake, miniature American Widgeon (baldpate) drake, miniature American Widgeon (baldpate) hen made by Captain Jobes.

Top left clockwise: full-size Ringed-neck drake, full-size Ringed-neck hen, miniature Ringed-neck drake, miniature Ringedneck hen made by Captain Jobes.

Left, Up-river Canvasback drake with wooden keel, Right, Up-river Canvasback hen with wooden keel made by Captain Jobes.

heads, Bailey Moltz did. There were six head whittlers that worked at Mitchell's and Bailey did ninety percent of the whittling. Ed Sampson draw knifed heads. You see, Mitchell only made decoys from September to November back in those days. I'm talking way before they started putting decoys on lamps for Christmas. It was only the last seven or eight years that Mr. Mitchell worked in that shop that it was open all year around.

"Mitchell influenced my style of making and painting of decoys. I prefer white pine and cedar for the bodies, white pine for the heads. Oil paints and Japan colors are blended for painting. I can paint a hundred decoys in a day. I've hand chopped a few decoys but not many. When I made my decoy machine in the seventies, Mitchell took one look at it and said it would never work. Hell, I can turn one hundred swan bodies in eight hours, by doing two at a time. All of the machines around here were made off of that machine.

"My three boys, Bobby, Charles, and Joey, make decoys. By the time next year rolls around they'll all have a shop of their own. I've taught them all I know but they still don't know it all yet. When it comes to making decoys they were just like a lab puppy; you throw it overboard and it swims. My wife Helen helps by sanding and puttying the bodies. She also paints the primer coat and takes care of the shipping. We send decoys all over the world.

"Ed Budnick is eighty-four years old and is my only employee and he is on the job every day.

"Bushwhacking is my favorite type of gunning. I used to set out two hundred decoys in my rig. The last time Mitchell bushwhacked, he was with me. There was one time in the fifties that six of us killed five hundred Canvasbacks in one week. I gunned a Remington automatic that held nine shells. It was later confiscated by the state game warden when I lent it to another boy to hunt with one time. I was never caught with it.

"Ed Cloke was a fellow who used to putty ducks for Mitchell. He also was a runner for Captain Jess Popular on his boat. Back in those times you didn't have outboards; you rowed around picking up cripples. There would be ten or fifteen on the water at a time. I've still got the old pair of ten gauge Greeners that came off Popular's boat.

"Mitchell would buy seven or eight cases of shotgun shells every year. When Eddy Mulden, 'Titbird,' Jimmy Pierce and myself would need shotgun shells he would say 'go get what you need and put them on the books.' He would take it out of what he owed you when you got paid.

"I have taken my boys gunning at one time or another over the years. Bobby was the only one I took bushwhacking because the others were too young when we quit.

"People who have never duck hunted before have no idea what it's like to see five hundred Canvasbacks fall out of the sky into your decoys when its snowing and just keep coming. I've seen them come in so close that they splashed water on me as I sculled by them and they looked me right in the eye. You try to bunch them together before you slap the side of the boat with the oar to get them up. The most ducks I pulled down in one scull was twenty-one fat Redheads. The wild celery on the flats and the Canvasbacks were what brought the millionaires here to gun. When the celery and grass was killed by the state because of complaints from the sail boaters, that's when the ducks left. It killed the hunting and fishing on the flats. The state put herbicide in the water to kill the grass but, it killed rock fish larvae by the acres. You could see it floating in big patches down the bay.

"Willie Parker has been on my boat to check me several times, but I knew when he was coming and where he was going before he got there. We had eyes on those flats. I sold a few ducks and swan in my time, but was never caught. The Canvasbacks went for as high as seven dollars a pair. The train would stop at Havre De Grace. We would put the ducks, feathers, guts, and all in the mail car. They would wind up in Philadelphia and New York in restaurants.

"Decoys have been a big part of life and always will."

Top, full-size Scoter drake. Middle, full-size Scoter hen. Left, miniature Scoter drake. Right, miniature Scoter hen made by Captain Jobes.

Top left clockwise: full-size Canvasback drake, full-size Canvasback hen, miniature Canvasback drake, miniature Canvasback hen made by Captain Jobes.

Top left clockwise: full-size Pintail hen, full-size Pintail drake, miniature Pintail hen, miniature Pintail drake made by Captain Jobes.

Top, full-size Black Ducks. Bottom, miniature Black Ducks made by Captain Jobes.

Top left clockwise: full-size Mallard drake, full-size Mallard hen, miniature Mallard drake, miniature Mallard hen made by Captain Jobes.

Top, Full-size Canada Goose. Bottom, miniature pair of Canada Geese by Captain Jobes.

Top, Full-size Snow Goose. Bottom, miniature pair of Snow Geese by Captain Jobes.

Top, Full-size Blue Goose. Bottom, miniature pair of Blue Geese by Captain Jobes.

Top, Full-size Brant. Bottom, miniature pair of Brant by Captain Jobes.

Top, Double headed American Coot. Middle, full-size American Coot. Bottom, miniature pair of American Coot by Captain Jobes.

Top, full-size Whistling (Tundra) Swan. Bottom, miniature pair of Whistling (Tundra) Swan by Captain Harry.

Top left clockwise: full-size Common Goldeneye hen, full-size Common Goldeneye drake, miniature Common Goldeneye drake and miniature Common Goldeneye hen made by Captain Jobes.

Top left clockwise: full-size Oldsquaw drake, full-size Oldsquaw hen, miniature American Oldsquaw hen and miniature Oldsquaw drake made by Captain Jobes.

Top left clockwise: full-size Redhead hen, full-size Redhead drake, miniature Redhead drake and miniature Redhead hen made by Captain Jobes.

Top left clockwise: full-size Northern Shoveler drake, full-size Northern Shoveler hen, miniature Northern Shoveler hen and miniature Northern Shoveler drake made by Captain Jobes.

Top left clockwise: full-size Blackhead hen, full-size Blackhead drake, miniature Blackhead drake, miniature Blackhead hen made by Captain Jobes.

Top left clockwise: full-size Bufflehead drake, full-size Bufflehead hen, miniature Bufflehead hen and miniature Bufflehead drake made by Captain Harry.

Top left clockwise: full-size Wood Duck drake, full-size Wood Duck hen, miniature Wood Duck hen and miniature Wood Duck drake made by Captain Jobes.

Top left clockwise: full-size Red-Breasted Merganser hen, full-size Red-Breasted Merganser drake, miniature Red-Breasted Merganser drake, miniature Red-Breasted Merganser hen made by Captain Jobes.

Top left clockwise: full-size Blue-winged Teal drake, full-size Blue-winged Teal hen, miniature Blue-winged Teal drake and miniature Blue-winged Teal hen made by Captain Harry.

Charles "Charlie" Jobes

"I was born February 28, 1968 in Havre de Grace, Maryland.

"My last year in high school I thought I wanted to be a welder. I had to be crazy. Welding is harder work than making decoys ever thought of being. After graduating I went to work for my dad (Capt'n Harry Jobes) part time and I fished with my brother Bobby on his boat for rock fish.

"I still have two of the first decoys I made at age seven. I made fifty or sixty miniature Canvasbacks and sold them at the Village of Cross Keys for fifty cents each. I sold them all! Man, did I think I was rich! People said, 'Sign them for me please.' I lived with my mother and she set up a little desk for me to use as a work bench. The eyes gave me a problem so I called my dad and asked him how to paint them. He said put a dot of red and a dot of black inside the red. I could not understand what he meant till I saw him do it. The decoys I made looked square back then but I tried to make them better each time.

"The decoys I make today are styled after my dad's. The way I learned to feather ducks was with him. He used to make little cast iron ducks for pen sets on a marble base. He would line up ninety five to a hundred on a rack, and there would be three or four racks full of them. He'd say, 'You sit there and I'll sit here.' I'd paint the white and put the feathers on the back while he would finish the rest. I know I painted a box car load of them. That's how I learned to paint. My brothers and I make decoys today because we like it not because we were pushed into it.

"My brother Bobby and I worked out an agreement that allowed me to work in his shop on my decoys. By the end of the year I'll have my own shop. I will be able to walk out my back door and go to work, or I can be late if I want. If I see something I want I just work a little harder and buy it.

"Bass wood, white pine and cedar are my favorite types of wood. The wood we get is mostly all new wood today. There aren't many cedar phone poles left anymore. In my dad's time the old cedar poles and pine barn beams made the bodies for most of the decoys. It didn't matter if the wood checked or cracked because they were going to be thrown into the water for gunning so you didn't worry about it. Now they go on a shelf and have to be as perfect as possible because people look them over real good.

"Bobby and I are having two machines built that will turn two bodies at one time. They will be built like our dads which is the best machine made. He made his own in 1972 or 1973. The standing geese and ducks that I make are the only handmade birds I make; all the rest have been machine made. I make half-size ducks and geese, full-size standing ducks and geese by myself. The full size decoys Bobby and I make together. Patty, my wife, takes care of finishing the eyes and bills. When I get my own shop the family will be together so we can watch the kids and work on decoys. I will not force decoys on my kids. However, if they want to learn, they will be taught the way my dad taught me.

"When I was working for my father I did a few things that Dad doesn't know about today. I was painting Mallard bills. You always give them two coats on the bills. Dad said, 'I'm going in the house and sit down for a while you put the second coat on those Mallard bills.' I got busy with something else when Bobby said, 'Here comes Dad and you never finished those Mallard bills.' When he walked in he looked at the Mallards and said, 'They look good, they look good.' He never knew I forgot to do them.

Another time I was painting my little miniatures on a cart in Dad's shop using black paint when I knocked the paint off on to the floor. Dad had seven or eight full-sized white Swans that had two or three coats of paint on them near by. The black paint covered every one of them with black spots. They looked like Dalmatian dogs. I started yelling for Bobby to come in here. 'What the heck are we going to do?' Bobby said, 'Don't worry about it. We'll clean them up. They still get two or three more coats of white paint yet.'

"The first time I hunted was with my brother Bobby and my dad, when I was about eight. We were in Doctor Currier's water blind on the Bohemia River. I was shooting a 410 gauge pump. One goose came in and swam next to the shore in the grass. Dad said, 'Shoot the goose in the head.' Ten minutes went by and I still couldn't see the goose, finally there it was and I missed it. Bobby got it on his third shot. I would have give anything to bushwhacked Canvasbacks with my dad but I know that can never happen now."

Charles "Charlie" Jobes paints half-size Canvasback drake. To the right of Charles is a full-size stand up Canada Goose. On painting table, left front clockwise: Half-size Pintail hen, Pintail drake, quarter-size Whistling (Tundra) Swan and Canvasback hen.

Patty Jobes is Charles's wife and helps him make decoys while raising a family.

Top center clockwise: full-size stand up Canada Goose, full-size stand up Mallard drake, half-size Mallard drake and full-size Mallard hen made by Charles "Charlie" Jobes.

Harry R. "Bobby" Jobes, Jr.

Harry R. "Bobby" Jobes Jr. paints yellow tear drop on miniature Whistling (Tundra) Swan. On table, left to right: miniature Mallard drake, miniature Mallard hen, miniature Snow Goose, miniature Common Goldeneye drake, miniature Common Goldeneye hen and full-size Blackhead drake made by him.

Debbie Jobes, Bobby's wife, also helps him with the decoy chores.

"I was born September 30, 1959 in Havre de Grace, Maryland.

"I graduated from high school in 1977 and went to work right away in Madison Mitchell's shop. I worked there for a year and then Mr. Mitchell sold his shop. After that I became a full-time waterman. I still continued to make decoys for my dad and Jimmy Pierce part-time. But being a waterman is a thing of the past. The water as a way of life is gone. There is just no money to be made. There is no money to be made because there are no fish or crabs left. The grass is gone from the water.

"If I had to place a blame for the lack of the grass, fish, and ducks I would have to say it was because of people. Humans are to blame. Back in the 60s the state came along and sprayed the grass because it was so thick. The environment is gone. Every where you look there are houses and roads, cars and people. People and their greed have ruined it. Not just one person or one factory, but people and their greed.

"Around 1980 I opened my own shop for decoy making. I made decoys before that, but not in my own shop. The first time I started making miniatures was down at Mr. Mitchell's. A fellow by the name of Norris Pratt came there. He had a 21 inch model of a bushwhack boat. He asked me if I could make him a gunning stool for his boat. I told him I could because at that time I was making these little ones about 1 ½ inches long. He brought me a bag full of wood cut in little squares. He said he would give me the wood to do it. I told him it would cost him a $1.00 a piece. I believe I made him about 100 little miniature Canvasbacks for his bushwhacking rig.

"I started making decoys because I grew up around it. As a kid I played down in the bottom of Mitchell's shop in the saw dust while Dad was upstairs painting decoys.

"Madison Mitchell, my dad, and Jimmy Pierce were the biggest influence in my style of carving. But all Jimmy Pierce's and my dad's are basically Madison Mitchell's style of paint job.

"I've changed the miniature patterns and the Wood duck patterns are our own. I blend my paint somewhat differently also. What I mean by that is it is not an ornamental blend and it is not a flat gunning blend. We do a little more stippling on them. No one particular carver influenced my style of painting. You look at different decoys and you get different ideas. Nobody ever makes a decoy on their own and can say this is my style. You always look at somebody's stuff and say 'That looks pretty good.' To me it's a combination of all styles blended together to come up with your own.

"I make my decoys from white pine wood, barn beams, cedar poles and bass wood. What ever is the best price at the right time. I don't use just one type of wood.

"For the paints I use the Japan colors mixed in with the oil based paints. I use some tube oil. That gives you a little bit of shine in some of the paint.

"Ninety per-cent of the bodies are done on machine. There are some that I do by hand. If I make a shore bird I will carve it by hand. I can carve a duck body as fast as the machine can carve it, but I can't do it all day long. It takes us about three-and-a-half to four minutes to turn out a duck body. The one machine we have will turn out miniatures to full-sized birds. From a Swan all the way down. We do full-size, miniatures and then there is the little tiny ones that are an inch long.

"I probably have made about five thousand gunning birds since I went into business for myself. As for the miniatures, it probably ranges to about a couple thousand a year.

"My wife used to help me a lot. She would prime, sand, take the orders for me. She is a very big part of it. But since we had our daughter she hasn't been able to help as much.

"We do have some fellows that work part-time during the busy times. They do the sanding, turning bodies. We have a couple of kids who have graduated from school and a couple of fellows who are retired. They come in and give us a hand doing a few things.

"Through the years I've strived to do better quality decoys. People buy decoys now for the quality. They really give them the once over and I don't blame them. When they used to come into Madison Mitchell's shop and pick up gunning decoys they would pile them in the trunk of the car, one on top of the other. They didn't care if they got scratched or nicked. Now you better not have a crack or a pin hole or anything in one of them today. I don't blame them though. They are paying about eight times as much for one now.

Miniature decoys by Bobby Jobes. Left front clockwise: Blackhead hen, Black Duck, Canvasback hen, Mallard drake, Black Swan, Canada Goose, Mallard hen, Canvasback drake, Black Duck, and Blackhead drake.

"My customers are gunners, collectors, anybody who wants them. Right now I am making fifty decoys for a man who lives in Cambridge. He's using Mallards, Pintails and he has three pairs of Wood Ducks that he is gunning.

"I started gunning when I was old enough to pick up a gun. We had an old twenty foot boat with a little cabin on it and I can remember my dad taking me out on it. There was a Coot swimming around. I had my 410 gun and I couldn't get it up to my shoulder. My dad kept on circling the Coot and I had to lay the butt of the gun up against the engine box and put my head down against the gun. I kept on trying to shoot this Coot and my dad kept going round and round in circles. I never did shoot the bird.

"Another time I remember was when we were bushwhacking down off of Davis's Hole. I used to sit up on the cabin of the boat and watch the decoys. This was in the middle of the day and every body was down in the cabin sleeping. They told me to let them know if any Canvasbacks came in. I was probably about six years old at the time. Well, this single Canvasback went into the decoys. Of course I didn't know what it was. So I told them a duck went into the decoys. My dad told me he was going to let me shoot the duck. Well I was scared to death. We went out there and started sculling through the decoys. I could hear the decoys hitting the side of the boat. My dad had to point the bird out to me. It was a drake Canvasback. I was so scared I didn't know what to do. I couldn't shoot my gun. My dad had to shoot it. That was the only time I can remember being in the bushwhack boat and having the opportunity to shoot a duck and I didn't do it.

"As a kid I gunned with my dad several times. He bushwhacked up until they closed Canvasbacks. After that he did a little bit of hunting but not a lot. I still enjoy body booting the best as compared to field hunting for geese. I can go right out my back door and go hunting. I don't have to drive an hour and a half and sit in a pit all day. I like to hunt on a cloudy, fall day. The best days are when it is dead calm. No wind. Not a ripple on the water. You can hear geese coming from a mile away.

"Now I hunt with my brother Charles. I have hunted some with my other brother Joey, but not as much as I have with Charles."

"There has been a lot of funny things that happened at Mitchell's shop. So many that it is hard to single out one. Bill Collins, 'Titbird' and me worked down there all the time. That would be around the 1970s. One time Michael Risinger walked up and was talking to 'Titbird.' 'Titbird' told him if he didn't shut up he was going to paint his tongue. He dared 'Titbird' to do it and opened his mouth. With that 'Titbird' stuck the paint brush in Michael's mouth. Like I said there was a lot of funny times. We always had good times when we worked there."

Joey Jobes

"I was born July 26, 1965 in Havre de Grace. After graduating from high school I commercial fished for a while with my older brother Bobby. Now I make decoys for a living.

"I started making decoys because the state put me out of business as far as fishing is concerned or I would probably still be fishing for a living. If I was a millionaire I would give my decoys away. I enjoy making decoys and I like the people that come in and buy them. But my first love is still fishing. When you went out and fished and came home with $50.00 in your hand you knew what you did for that money.

"Probably the first decoy I made was when I was about seven years old. When I was around five or six years old I carved, puttied, primed, and sanded. This of course was in my dad's shop. I guess you could say I played with the decoys because Dad was decoy carving. I worked for my dad for as long as I could. I didn't expect him to hand me anything, but I just had to have more money.

"I started my own shop in the summer of '87. I didn't want to start my own place till I had all the equipment that I would need. I was working at Pat Vincenti's shop at the time. We were putting together about 200 Teal. I would draw knife the heads and Pat would carve them. Then I would finish sanding them. I had all the bodies ready and most of the heads ready. I went up there next day to sand Teal heads. There was two bushel baskets of them. When I got there he didn't have them whittled. He had me raking and doing things that had nothing to do with making decoys. I went back the next day and he still didn't have them whittled. I told him I would come back the next day. The first thing I did was come right to my shop and started getting things together. I went to Lennie Ferguson's and bought a bunch of bodies. I got a bunch of head wood that was hard as a rock and whittled Canvasback heads. I was still determined not to make decoys full time until I had everything and was ready. So back to Pat's I went the next day. He still didn't have those heads whittled. I went back home and set up shelves. I got into making those ducks and I never went back to Pat's. I guess I owe it to Pat for helping me make the decision to start on my own as soon as I did.

Joey Jobes whittles duck head. Unfinished decoy sets to his right, while previously gunned over Blackhead drake sets in foreground.

Left, Joey Jobes holding 10 gauge Greener double barrel shotgun from Captain Jess Popular. Center, Charles Jobes in dry diving suit used for body-booting. Right, Bobby Jobes holds Blackhead drake.

Top center clockwise: full-size Whistling (Tundra) Swan, Bufflehead drake, and Canvasback drake made by Mr. Jobes.

"There were three people who influenced my style of decoy carving. They were Madison Mitchell, my dad (Capt'n Harry Jobes) and Pat Vincenti. When I lived at home I had a lamp that Madison Mitchell made. It was a Blue-winged Teal hen. He had given the lamps to my mother for a wedding present. I would go to bed at night and look at that Teal. Look at the way it was shaped and the tail, the breast and how he got that head on there. When I make a pattern for my lathe now I try to get some of the things in there that I think will work better. My dad would show me the fast way because he could really put out the ducks. Pat Vincenti showed me how to take my time and get things a little more right.

"I use white pine for the heads of my decoys and mostly white pine for the bodies. Once in a while I will use bass wood. If I get a good piece of poplar I will use that. They are all machine made. None have ever been hand-chopped. I'm turning bodies on my own lathe. I use all oil base paint and mix my own colors.

"Since I started in business for myself I have probably made between 1,500 and 2,000 decoys. My customers are mainly collectors. A lot of them gun but they don't use my decoys for gunning.

"I have never employed anybody but I have taught a couple of people. Not everything that they know now, but I did help to get them started. I sold Chris Hawkins the first duck bodies he ever had. I got him started making decoys. I've got the first miniature swan Chris ever made. I also taught Pat Vincenti a few tricks of the trade. But you got to remember I learned from my dad and Madison Mitchell. Pat's first decoys never had nails in the heads. He would glue them on.

"My favorite duck to gun was the Canvasback. I also enjoy gunning for Blackheads. I first started hunting when I was about six years old. I went out with my father body-booting. We would get down there in the morning. He would have that old boat and it wouldn't start half of the time. I would just pray for that boat to start because I didn't want to go to school.

"I've hunted a lot with Dave Wooten. He knows what I do, I know what he does. Right now I enjoy hunting with him a lot. We've body-booted, the pit, just all types of gunning. I've gone body-booting with him when nobody else would take me. Dave Turner is another one I like to hunt with.

"The one hunt that sticks out in my mind was when I was about thirteen years old. We went body-booting with my dad one day. We were getting at the age where we could shoot a gun by ourselves. It was Charles, my father and me. Charles and my father got in the aluminum boat and they put out a few sets of frames. My father told me to take the boat and go a long way from them but keep them in sight. When they waved I was to go to them. About an hour went by and I was starting to get sleepy. I said to myself, 'The hell with it. I'm going to sleep.' I didn't see anything wrong with going to sleep. You know how when you are sleeping you can hear something that doesn't quite wake you up. Well, I kept hearing this noise and about fifteen minutes later I woke up and realized that it was a gun shot. He and Charles wanted me to put up the dead birds. When I got there he gave me hell. I didn't realize that it could be dangerous not to be watching out for them. Fog, wind and tides could have put them in real trouble. Anything could have happened and I would not have known it."

Charles W. "Speed" Joiner, Jr.

"I was born in Betterton, Maryland on July 19, 1921. I inherited the nickname of 'Speed' from my father. Where he got it, who knows.

"I worked for the power company as a lineman for nearly 20 years. Then, after I had an accident and nearly knocked my brains out, they made me manager. I was a manager at the power company for about 20 more years."

"I started making decoys out of necessity. I couldn't afford to buy them so I started making them. I guess I was about 20 years old when I began making decoys. I had always fooled with decoys long before that. I was living with my grandmother in Betterton and I would come home on weekends. I had a little shop at her place. Shortly after I began making decoys I cut out some silhouette goose decoys. I worked on them that summer, figuring on using them that fall. I took them back with me to Haver de Grace to paint them in the evenings and discovered I didn't know anything about it. So I asked the Springers, people I lived with in Havre de Grace who I should see. They sent me to Madison Mitchell's shop. He got me started. Madison painted a couple for me and then he set me down at the table and turned me loose.

"There was something about Madison's place that fascinated me. I was always interested in decoy making, like I said before, but I had never seen an operation like Madison's. So I kept going back and tried to learn a little bit at a time. All of 1942 I hung around Madison's shop. Ed Sampson, Eddie Mauldin, Pete Whitey and a guy they called Smitty worked there. They had what appeared like an assembly line going. Then I went in the service during the war. When I came home, Madison told me to go upstairs in the back room of his shop and that there was something up there for me. My God, there was a pile of decoys about four feet high. Madison had saved a lot of junk bodies and patched decoys for me.

Charles "Speed" Joiner finishes painting a Canvasback drake while Canvasback hen rests on table. In background on left hangs a pair of his full-size flat bottom Wood Ducks.

Selected as Honorary Chairman for the Havre de Grace Decoy Festival in 1987, Speed Joiner stands with his collection of full-size decoys sold at the auction.

Charles "Speed" Joiner stands with his collection of miniature decoys sold at the auction.

"Before I went into the service Madison and I used to gun together and when I came back home we continued for years to gun. We developed a close relationship.

"I guess Madison Mitchell was the one who influenced me in my style for a number of years until I met the Ward brothers. I still continued to paint some like Madison, but I also picked up some of the Ward brothers painting style and carvings. The Havre de Grace style is more durable and easier to reproduce. You could turn out hundreds and hundreds of them, whereas the Ward brother's decoys are all handmade. They are not machine made at all. They may be a little more realistic looking, but you can't turn out hundreds of them.

"The Havre de Grace decoys were machine made. The open water was rougher and the round bottom bird worked the best in the upper bay. People had big rigs. If they were going to run the Flats they would have maybe 250-500 decoys to a rig. Well, over here on the Eastern Shore, nobody used a rig that big. It's just a different type of gunning altogether.

"My style of painting is a combination of Madison Mitchell's and the Ward brother's. It depends on what I'm doing. Some species, for instance the Canvasback, that's Madison's style. For most of the rest of the decoys I have gotten away from that style.

"The best wood for a gunning and durable decoy is western red cedar. Anymore, today, I make them out of bass wood, tupelo gum and white pine. For head woods I use mostly white pine.

"For painting, on my working decoys, I use mostly yacht paints. For the miniatures and the more decorative decoys I use tube colors, the regular oils.

"In the earlier times I hand-chopped a few of the birds. All my swans today are handmade. In fact, some of the flat bottoms I make today are all handmade. The only machine made ducks I make are the round bottom. As far as fancy decorative decoys go I have used a Foredom tool on several pairs where I have burned some feathers in them. There may still be some of them around in the states somewhere, but I know that there is a couple pair of them going to England. It would be hard to say how many decoys I have made. Probably about 20,000 would be a conservative guess for gunning birds. I wouldn't even want to make a guess as to how many miniatures I have made.

"When I lived in Betterton and was repairing and repainting stools for gun clubs, Nelson Crew and Nelson Boone used to help me at night. Some years I did nearly a thousand birds by machine. For a couple of years we kept track of cripples. We would average about fifteen hundred a year. Out of them you might do 75 re-heads and re-paints.

"As far as passing decoy making to the next generation, I guess it would be my nephew Billy Joiner. I also helped Dave Blackiston, Bob Coleman, Barry Fuchs and Bill Schauber get started.

"All of my customers early on were all gunners. Various times I

Mr. Joiner takes time to sign one of his decoys for a young collector at the Havre de Grace Decoy Festival in 1987.

have gotten orders for five to ten dozen decoys, mainly diving ducks from gun clubs and farms. I guess my best known customers were Ted Williams, Senator Muskie and Bob Carpenter. Bob Carpenter, I believe, at one time owned the Philadelphia Phillies.

"I believe I started hunting as soon as I could stand up. Seems like I hunted all my life. Started out hunting small game. I didn't get into duck hunting until I was about 16 years old. My father and brother didn't hunt. I hunted some with an uncle. When I started with waterfowl hunting it was with two other boys my age, Lawrence Price and Jim Owens. We gunned together for quite a few years. When we first started out hunting we used gallon Prestone antifreeze cans painted black. All we had coming in was Black Ducks, sometimes Pintails and a few Baldpates.

"I used to walk the shores at Betterton and pick up decoys that would break loose from the Flats. The northwest winds would set them right on the shore. Sometimes you could pick up a half dozen. That's how we got our rig to gun Canvasbacks.

"When we started out gunning, the other two fellows I mentioned, myself, and a fellow I worked with rented a farm. We could rent a whole farm for $200.00 a year. Which back then was a lot of money. But we had the whole farm for upland game, goose shooting in the field and duck shooting on the shore.

"My favorite species of duck is the Canvasback. I don't know why except that it seemed like more fun and of course you had better shooting. And there was a lot more of it. Black Ducks were a little wary. For the Black Ducks we had a blind in the creek on shore. You know, you have to build a Black Duck blind out of two inch plank. The reason for that is, a Black Duck can see through a one inch plank. For Canvasback we used a stake blind out in the water. They're also known as a "booby" blind. I used to goose hunt too, mostly in pits, all around Betterton. Most of the time we would put out around 200 decoys for ducks. We mixed up everything Redheads, Canvasbacks and Blackheads. All diving ducks. We would kill all three species. No puddle ducks. Very rarely would you ever get a Black Duck or a puddle duck.

"For goose hunting we had several different kind of decoys. At first we started off with silhouettes made out of plywood. Then the next thing that came out was the Johnson's folding decoys. They were actually a photograph that was glued to cardboard. Then we went to the shell type and then the solid bodies. I made about 50 or 60 wooden ones of my own that were turned out on a machine. They were round bottomed with weights and pegs in the bottom of them. We could use them in the field or use them overboard.

"I had a gunning dog. A Chesapeake Retriever. I got him in 1946. I gunned him about 10 years and retired him. We both retired gunning at the same time. I quit gunning because I had a different feeling toward shooting game. I guess the thing that stands out most in my mind was one time I shot and crippled a goose. That kind of put the icing on the cake. Running that goose down in skim ice got to me. As I was rowing after it I got to thinking about all the times it had beat it's way back and forth from here to Canada and then to die a death like that for our sport. I quit right then and there. I never went again from that day to this. I still enjoy the taste of game but I just don't want to kill any of it.

"I have had so many memorable hunts it's hard to pick out one particular one.

"I have outlawed. Didn't do anything but that for the first four or five years. I never sold birds. Never wasted any of the game. Always put them to use. I had been checked out quite a few times by game wardens but there was never any problem. The only time I was picked up was by the Feds for baiting. It happened the last year I hunted. The Feds said we had baited for ducks. What they found was not put out by anyone there on that farm. It had come from across the creek someplace. It was barley chafe. It was in the driftwood and seaweed at high tide line. That was what they wrote us up for. They dragged a scoop in the water in front of our blind but, never did find any grain overboard. But that is over and done with.

"When I hunted I used a Remington Model 11 gun. One of the old ones made off of a Browning patent.

"Madison Mitchell was very particular about his decoy carvings. One of the things that always stuck in my mind was when he was teaching me to whittle heads. When you picked up a head to whittle you would start at the same place and you would finish in the same place. I guess if he and I were to whittle today we would both start in the same place and finish in the same cut.

"I was taking heads home with me like a bushel basket at one time. When I would get them done I would bring them back to the shop. Every time I took them back he would look at them and pick them apart. He would say I either cut too much out of here or hadn't cut enough out there. But he would tell me not to worry, that he could straighten 'em up with a sander when he went to sand them. One night, after this had gone on for several times, I took a basket of heads back into the shop that I had been working on. When I went through the shop I picked one out of the basket he had done. I took it upstairs and asked Madison: 'How's that?' He looked at it and started picking it apart. When he got done I said, 'Well, that's one you did.' I think when he looked away I could see him kind of grinning to himself. I figured if he couldn't tell mine from his I must be doing okay."

Mr. Joiner uses a draw knife on decoy head.

Mr. Joiner whittles the bill on decoy head.

Decoy body is held firmly by decoy vise while Mr. Joiner uses wood rasp to shape breast.

"Starting to look like a decoy now" said Mr. Joiner as he nails on the head.

Charles "Speed" Joiner used two Wood Duck patterns over the years. Top left, pattern number 2 of full-size flat bottom Wood Duck drake with wood keel. Top right, pattern number 2 of full-size flat bottom Wood Duck hen with wood keel. Middle left, pattern number 2 of miniature Wood Duck drake. Middle right, pattern number 2 of miniature Wood Duck hen. Bottom left, pattern number 1 of miniature Wood Duck drake. Bottom right, pattern number 1 of miniature Wood Duck hen.

Full-size cork Canada Goose by Mr. Joiner.

Top left clockwise: full-size Black Duck drake, full-size Black Duck hen, miniature Black Duck hen and miniature Black Duck drake made by Mr. Joiner.

Top left clockwise: full-size Blackhead drake, full-size Blackhead hen, miniature Blackhead hen and miniature Blackhead drake made by Mr. Joiner.

Top left clockwise: full-size American Widgeon (Baldpate) drake, full-size American Widgeon (Baldpate) hen, miniature American Widgeon (Baldpate) hen and miniature American Widgeon (Baldpate) drake made by Mr. Joiner.

Top, full-size Brant. Bottom, miniature Brant made by Charles "Speed" Joiner.

Top, full-size Whistling (Tundra) Swan. Bottom, miniature made by Whistling (Tundra) Swan Mr. Joiner.

Top left clockwise: full-size flat bottom Pintail drake with wood keel, full-size flat bottom Pintail hen with wood keel, miniature Pintail hen and miniature Pintail drake made by Mr. Joiner.

Top left clockwise: full-size flat bottom Green-winged Teal drake with wood keel, full-size flat bottom Green-winged Teal hen with wood keel, miniature Green-winged Teal hen and miniature Green-winged Teal drake made by Mr. Joiner.

Top left clockwise: full-size Mallard drake, full-size Mallard hen, miniature Mallard hen and miniature Mallard drake made by Mr. Joiner.

Left clockwise: full-size Redhead drake, full-size Redhead hen, miniature Redhead hen and miniature Redhead drake made by Mr. Joiner.

Top left clockwise: full-size Canvasback drake, full-size Canvasback hen, miniature Canvasback hen and miniature Canvasback drake made by Mr. Joiner.

Top left clockwise: full-size flat bottom Common Goldeneye drake with wood keel, full-size flat bottom Common Goldeneye hen with wood keel, miniature Common Goldeneye hen and miniature Common Goldeneye drake made by Mr. Joiner.

Top, full-size American Widgeon (Baldpate) drake sleeper. Bottom, full-size American Widgeon (Baldpate) hen sleeper by Charles "Speed" Joiner.

Top, full-size Canvasback) drake sleeper. Bottom, full-size Canvasback hen sleeper by Mr. Joiner.

Top, full-size Canada Goose. Bottom, miniature Canada Goose made by Mr. Joiner.

Top, cast iron Canvasback drake sinkbox decoy. Bottom, cast iron Canvasback hen sinkbox decoy painted by Mr. Joiner and were sold by Orvis Company in the mid 80's.

Top, decorative flat bottom Canvasback drake. Bottom, decorative flat bottom Canvasback hen made by Charles "Speed" Joiner.

Full-size decorative Whistling (Tundra) Swan made by Mr. Joiner. Elegance in decoy collecting.

Mr. Joiner is shown putting out Canvasback decoys for the last time. Scene was created on the Chester river for the cover of the Havre de Grace Festival book in 1987.

View of full-size Canvasback drake decoy shows a number 2 branded in the bottom. This two inch brand marked all decoys that Speed Joiner sold as seconds. "I didn't make many. When I had blocks that had a little creosote in them or were knotty I saved them for myself. The creosote would eventually come through the paint. Hunters would ask me to sell them. I branded them as seconds and sold them for half price with no guarantee. At those prices ($2.50) I didn't want to see them come back."

Pair of Mr. Joiner's Canvasback drakes are at work off Millers Island.

Decorative Pintail drake made by Mr. Joiner.

Steven "Steve" Lay puts the eyes on a full-size Canvasback drake while full-size Mallard drake sits on table.

Steven "Steve" Richard Lay

"I was born on October 18, 1951 in Havre de Grace, Maryland. I went to Harford Community College for two years. I finished my education at Cincinnati College of Mortuary Science in Cincinnati, Ohio. I passed my National Board of Exam and my Maryland State Exam back in 1975. I worked in the funeral business for a couple of years. Then I decided that if I could spend as much time and effort into working for myself as a waterman I could make as much money and be much happier. Although things have changed on the Bay in the last 12 to 15 years I still enjoy it.

"I was fifteen years old when I started making decoys. My father had worked for Madison Mitchell and he had a lamp at home that had a duck on it. That duck on that lamp looked so real I would almost have to touch every day to remind me that it was made of wood. I thought that was really neat. I was beginning to get an interest in the outdoors so my father took me down to Mr. Mitchell's and showed me around. Mr. Mitchell hired me to work for him in the summers and after school. At about that same time my dad took me down to Jim Pierce's where I also began working for Jim.

"Mr. Mitchell taught me how to make decoys and I picked up the painting from Mr. Pierce.

"I use the cedar wood for the antique duck, which is becoming quite popular. Also bass wood is becoming a very popular wood to use, especially for me, because it doesn't have the sap and the knots that the pine does.

"I use all oil base paints, Rustoleum basically to start with. The tools that I use are pretty standard for what the Havre de Grace style has been. The draw knife, band saws, router. I get my bodies from Lenny Ferguson or J. K. Pierce turns me some hand-sized stuff. I do not have a machine. But they are turned bodies. Everything I make is round bottomed. I guess right now I make about four to five hundred decoys a year.

"My wife helps me a little bit. And so does my father. Once in a while if some guys want to help do a little something they do, but other than that I have no help.

"I haven't made any changes in my decoy making since I first started. It is still basically what Mr. Mitchell and Mr. Pierce taught me.

"The majority of my customers are collectors and dealers. A few people do gun my decoys. There is one guy down on the western shore near Annapolis who guns my decoys and I send some to the Carolinas every year to a couple of guys who do gun them.

"I started hunting when I was about 15 years old, mainly waterfowl on the Flats. I have gone over to the Eastern Shore with a couple of friends when I began hunting geese. But basically I was interested in hunting the ducks out here on the Flats. The style of hunting I did was body booting. I never bushwhacked. I have been hunting with Brian Bailey since day one.

"The most memorable encounter was with Mr. Mitchell. I worked for him for fifteen years from 1965 to 1980 when he closed his shop. Last day there he called me up on the phone and told me to come over to his house. It was in the winter around Christmas. He gave me my last pay check and said he had decided to close his shop. It was really a tough moment for me to handle after all the years I had been with him. That is certainly a day I will never forget. It was very sad and I'm sure both of us cried at the time too.

"When I was working for Mr. Mitchell, Ed Cloak was there along with Ed Sampson, Jimmy Pierce, Jobey and Eddie Mauldin."

Left front clockwise: Full-size Mallard drake, full-size Canvasback hen, full-size Canada Goose swimmer, full-size Canvasback drake, and full-size Mallard hen made by Mr. Lay.

Robert G. "Bob" Litzenberg

"I was born July 27 1910 in Elkton, Maryland. Graduated from Elkton High School in 1930.

"The first job I had after high school was in a grocery store making thirteen dollars for a six day week. That job lasted for three years till I asked for a raise and was told 'no, he can't afford it.' I borrowed one hundred dollars from my father and started my own meat business. The first side of beef I bought cost me thirty dollars for three hundred pounds from Swift and Company. I sold the round steaks for nineteen cents a pound and T-bone sold for twenty-nine cents a pound. I gave up the meat business after three years. My brother Bill and I built a restaurant on the edge of our farm to feed the people at the Navy Explosives Plant that was being built. We served up to two thousand meals a day. I cooked seven crates of eggs (one crate equals 30 dozen eggs) for breakfast every week. All of our platters had a ceiling price of forty cents. I got drafted into the service during World War II and was sent to Korea. When I came back after the war my brother and I sold the restaurant and went into the painting business.

"My brother and I bought a rail bird skiff for twenty dollars to gun out of when we were teenagers. We would gun in the Elk Marsh for rail birds and ducks. At that time we had live decoys to gun over also. I bought forty unpainted canvasback decoys, forty Blackhead and Redhead decoys for forty and fifty cents each from Mr. Norris Pratt. Over the years they got lost when we loaned them out. We would gun on the flats and the North East River. Back then you could take a coffee pot and dip the water for our coffee right out of the river, it was that clear and clean. In those times the North East River was the best in the state for large mouth bass. Now, as we know, it has all changed.

"I gunned the sinkbox on the flats with Walter Blair the last time before they outlawed it. He was the son of John Blair, the famous decoy maker. I could never afford to hire a sinkbox back then. It cost one to two hundred dollars a day to rent a sinkbox. That was a lot of money during the Depression years. A man who owned two

Robert "Bob" G. Litzenberg puts eye on Pintail drake. Finished high-neck Canvasback hen and drake are on his right. Robert "Bob" G. Litzenberg was selected as Honorary Chairman for the Havre de Grace Decoy Festival in 1984. A complete collection of Litzenberg decoys were sold at auction.

Red-breasted Merganser by Bob Litzenberg.

Top, Pintail hen. Bottom, Pintail drake by Mr. Litzenberg.

Pair of American Coots by Mr. Litzenberg.

Pidgeon by Bob Litzenberg.

Top, Green-winged Teal hen. Bottom, Green-winged Teal drake by Mr. Litzenberg.

drugstores would rent it and take Walter and I with him. Three people were necessary to gun the sinkbox. You would have to tow the box out and put out five to six hundred decoys. Depending on the weather it could take up to three hours to take up all those decoys. A bushwhacking rig took one man rowing and two men winding decoys however, it would only take twenty minutes to pick up one hundred twenty-five decoys. That's winding and never letting up.

"I guess I preferred the bushwhacking the most. It was harder to shoot when the boat would be bouncing up and down. The best time to gun was after a front came through and the wind was from the northwest. It just set the canvasbacks crazy. I never sold a duck in my life, but I can say I've killed my share. He was the best eating duck on the bay. We used to average about six hundred canvasbacks a season.

"My favorite shotgun was an old Remington made off of the Browning patents. The last time I gunned was in the sixties but I still own the gun. I can say I saw the flats at their best in those days.

"The sinkbox, bushwhack boat and the rail bird skiff were given by my brother and I to the Upper Bay Museum at North East, Maryland.

"I made my first decoys to gun over in 1930 when I was twenty years old. One hundred canvasbacks were made similar to Will Heverin's decoys. Heverin's decoys always looked the best to me. The decoys I made were from old wood taken from barn beams that were white pine. All the decoys I made have been hand-chopped with a hatchet. From there I use a draw knife, and spokeshave. We didn't have any sanders back in those times, what little sanding there was we did by hand. I use outside oil base paints for everything I do.

"I've made hundreds of decoys but I could not tell you exactly how many. I would have to guess it would be around five hundred decoys in all. I know I have donated and given several hundred decoys away. The collection I made for the Havre de Grace Decoy show sold for seven thousand four hundred dollars at the auction. I made a set of heads, one of each species I make for a special auction. They sold for five thousand six hundred dollars. All the proceeds were donated to the Havre de Grace Decoy Museum. Dr. Frank Capanegro and his wife were my best customers. One of the greatest men I ever met in my life. He bought both of my collections that I mentioned. I only got to meet him about six years ago. He died about six weeks after he bought the head collection. I miss him more than any other man I've met in my life."

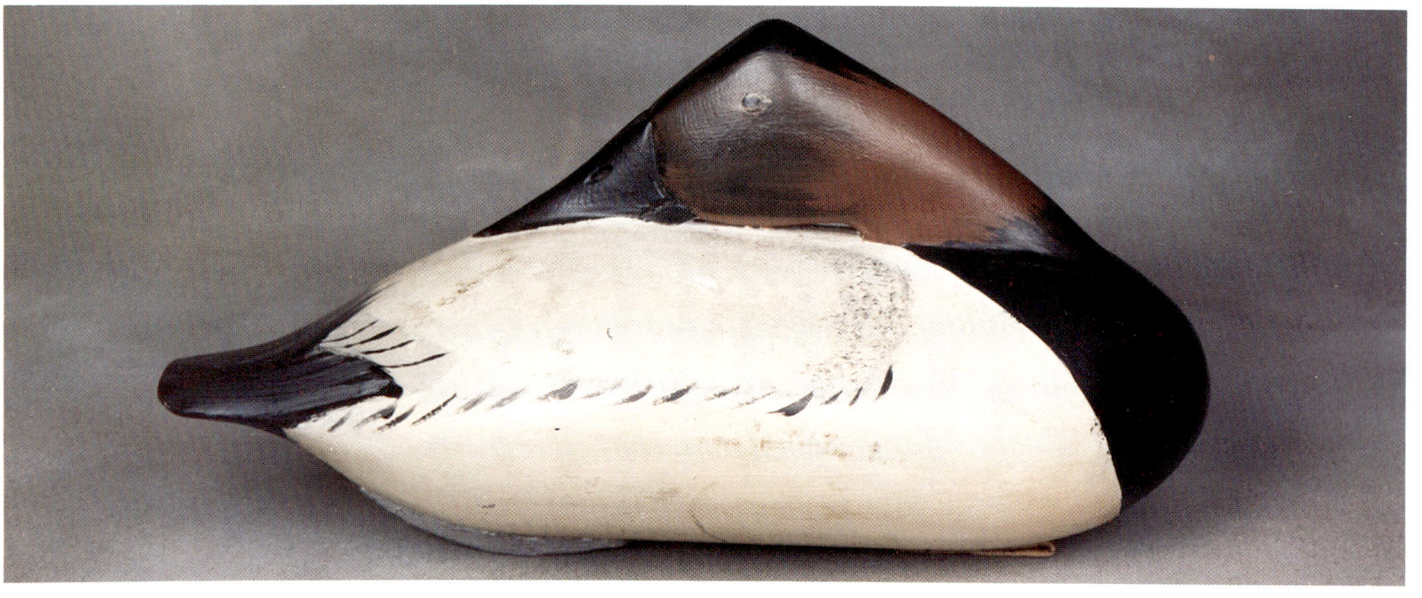

Canvasback drake sleeper by Mr. Litzenberg.

American Widgeon (Baldpate) by Bob Litzenberg.

Top, Blue-winged Teal drake. Bottom, Blue-winged Teal hen by Mr. Litzenberg.

Top, Ruddy Duck hen. Bottom, Ruddy Duck drake by Mr. Litzenberg.

Black Duck by Bob Litzenberg.

Great Blue Heron by Mr. Litzenberg.

Canada Goose swimmer by Mr. Litzenberg.

Curlew by Mr. Litzenberg.

Blue Goose by Mr. Litzenberg.

Rail by Mr. Litzenberg.

Canada Goose by Mr. Litzenberg.

Snow Goose by Bob Litzenberg.

Cinnamon Teal drake sleeper by Mr. Litzenberg.

Cinnamon Teal hen sleeper by Mr. Litzenberg.

Blue-winged Teal drake sleeper by Mr. Litzenberg.

Blue-winged Teal hen sleeper by Mr. Litzenberg.

Top, wood Canvasback hen sinkbox decoy. Bottom, wood Canvasback drake sinkbox decoy by Mr. Litzenberg.

Top, Canvasback hen. Bottom, Canvasback drake by Bob Litzenberg.

Top, Bufflehead hen sleeper. Bottom, Bufflehead drake sleeper by Mr. Litzenberg.

Top, Bufflehead hen. Bottom, Bufflehead drake by Mr. Litzenberg.

Top, cast iron Canvasback hen sinkbox decoy. Bottom, cast iron Canvasback drake sinkbox decoy by Mr. Litzenberg.

Top, Common Goldeneye hen. Bottom, Common Goldeneye drake by Mr. Litzenberg.

Top, Redhead hen. Bottom, Redhead drake by Mr. Litzenberg.

Top, Northern Shoveler hen. Bottom, Northern Shoveler drake by Bob Litzenberg.

Top, decorative Blackhead hen. Bottom, decorative Blackhead drake by Mr. Litzenberg.

Top, Blackhead hen. Bottom, Blackhead drake by Mr. Litzenberg.

Top, highneck Canvasback hen. Bottom, highneck Canvasback drake by Mr. Litzenberg.

Top, Mallard hen. Bottom, Mallard drake by Mr.Litzenberg.

Bob Litzenberg (left) and Allen Purner (right) re-enact "Rail Bird hunting on Little Elk Creek" for cover of the Havre de Grace Decoy Festival book in 1986.

William "Bill" Litzenberg
Born: 1908 lived in Elkton, Cecil County, Maryland
Died: 1975

Full-size Blackhead drake by William "Bill" Litzenberg.

Full-size Blackhead hen by Bill Litzenberg.

George Lockard
Born: 1866 lived in Elk Neck, Cecil County, Maryland
Died: 1931

Full-size Canvasback drake made by George Lockard.

Henry Lockard
Born: 1868 lived in Elk Neck, Cecil County, Maryland
Died: 1944

Full-size Redhead drake made by Henry Lockard.

Robert "Bob" Lord holds Canvasback drake. To his right sits a Canvasback hen with Blackhead drake behind it.

Robert "Bob" Frances Lord

"I was born April 9, 1917 in Preston, Maryland. After I graduated from high school, and as a boy, I did all types of work associated with farming. Then in July, 1937, I went to work for the telephone company. I worked for the phone company until I retired in July, 1979.

"I was about thirty years old when I started making decoys. It was January, 1947. I made them on my own. We had a blind on the Chesapeake Bay, just above Eastern Neck Island. A few boys I gunned with and myself had a few decoys. We put up some booby blinds. We couldn't gun too often down there because the water would get so rough. We had a few decoys that we kept in the blinds. We were out there one day and it was real rough. We had put our decoys out. Our decoys were a few wooden ones and some Carry Lites. You know those Carry Lites are only made of plastic. When we took them up after a hunt one day and we set the wooden ones on top of the Carry Lites. It was several days before we hunted again and when we did the wooden ones had collapsed the Carry Lights flat. That's when I decided I was going to make some wooden decoys.

"When I first started I used a hatchet and white cedar wood. I split my pieces and kind of squared them up. Then I drew my pattern on the wood and started chopping. I chopped all day and by night time I couldn't see over the pile of chips and my arms were so sore I could hardly lift them to feed myself. When it was all done that first day I had chopped out twelve decoys. I still have three or four of them left today. The rest have gotten away from me through the years.

"That evening I walked down to the hardware store and a fellow came in and wanted a couple of keys made. I watched the man in there cut out the keys and I thought to myself I probably could make a machine that would do the same thing with decoys. So I made my machine on the same principle as a key machine with a pattern decoy. From that I made improvements on it till I had it to where you could cut a Canvasback decoy in six minutes. Also, you would have very little work to do to it when it came off the machine.

"Through the years I guess I have made about twenty-five hundred decoys. It paid what expenses I had for my gunning. I really didn't make them to go into a business. I turned a lot of bodies for Jess Urie. He had a real big business in decoy making and at that time he didn't have a machine. He copied one from mine later on. His son Roger had gone in the service and he was behind in his orders and that's how I come about making the blanks for him. I guess for the two years I did that for Jess, I must have made about a thousand bodies.

"I would take and modify some decoys that I liked. Whose they were I have no way of knowing. We would walk the shore and pick up decoys that were washed down from the Susquehanna River.

"My style of painting was more or less my own. There are two ways of painting decoys. One style is for gunning and the other is for show. I even put eyes on mine. I used a twenty-two caliber bullet with a little bit of red and yellow paint on the end of it. It would make the prettiest pair of eyes. At first I used a regular outdoor flat house paint for my decoys. Then about 1950 I switched to the acrylic paints.

"Around 1962 I slowed down making my decoys. At that time I had been transferred to Easton in my work and I didn't have time. Also, they had come out with some real nice plastic and neoprene decoys for gunning about that time. The manufacturers could make them much cheaper than we could sell them for. Plus they were a lot lighter to carry.

"My wife helped me turn the bodies in the early days before I put the self-feeder on the machine. She would cut a lot of blanks while I was away working. You really didn't have to do anything but put the decoy in the machine and turn it on.

"I started waterfowl hunting back in 1946. This was when I was living in Chestertown. One day I went goose hunting with Jimmy Williams. That was the first time I had ever been goose hunting. I really enjoyed it. I loved the Canvasback. That's about as good an eating bird as you can find. Actually I enjoyed them all. Even the little old Ruddy Duck. That was back when it was legal to bait for them. I say it was legal to the point that the state would let you bait up to two hundred yards of the blind, but the federal said it was illegal.

"I had, in my opinion, one of the finest Chesapeake Bay Retrievers. Her name was Bonnie. That dog had more sense than a lot of the fellows I gunned with. If we were crawling along the fence posts she would crawl right along with you. She wouldn't move till I fired the gun and then you better watch out. She would dive out of sight in the water for the Canvasbacks and get every one of them. One time there was several fellows from Westinghouse were gunning with me and we had winged a Pintail and the duck dove under the water. I told the fellows watch that dog dive for that duck. They didn't believe me. Well, she dived and brought back the duck. She would get two at a time some times. She would bring a cripple and then go back for the dead ones with out being told to do it. She knew what it was all about and was one of the smartest dogs I have ever seen. I didn't train her. It just seemed to be instinct.

"The gun I used, so they tell me, is a collector's item. It is a Remington 870 Pump with a 877 barrel. I believe there was only about four hundred of them ever made. I still have it. I bought back in 1948 from a sporting goods store in Dover, Delaware.

"I haven't done any decoy making since 1962. But maybe I can get myself together and scrounge out something and give to the Havre de Grace Museum."

Top left clockwise, full-size Blackhead drake, full-size Canvasback hen and full-size Canvasback drake made by Mr. Lord.

Robert F. "Bob" McGaw
Born: 1879 lived in Havre De Grace, Harford County, Maryland
Died: 1958

Miniature Whistling (Tundra) Swan by Bob McGaw.

Top, miniature Mallard hen. Bottom, miniature Mallard drake by Robert "Bob" F. McGaw.

Miniature Black Duck by Mr. McGaw.

Top, miniature Redhead hen. Bottom, miniature Redhead drake by Mr. McGaw.

Top, miniature Canvasback hen. Bottom, miniature Canvasback drake by Mr. McGaw.

Top, miniature Blackhead hen. Bottom, miniature Blackhead drake by Mr. McGaw.

Two miniature feeding Canada geese by Bob McGaw.

Top, miniature Pintail hen. Bottom, miniature Pintail drake by Mr. McGaw.

Full-size Black Duck by Mr. McGaw.

Full-size Canvasback drake by Bob McGaw.

Full-size Canvasback hen by Mr. McGaw.

Full-size Black Duck "Tipper" by Mr. McGaw.

Joseph Evans McKinney

"I was born May 21, 1913 in Elkton, Maryland.

"I graduated from high school and then went two years to a preparatory school. The only reason I could go was that the head master needed his grass mowed. I mowed the grass in the spring and fall and that paid for my tuition. I received a scholarship to Johns Hopkins. I attended there for two years.

"In the summer of '35 I went to work for the Corps of Engineers at Chesapeake City as a surveyor. Chesapeake City came under the Corps of Engineers of Philadelphia so we had all of the Delaware coast line. I helped survey all those little creeks from Christiania to Indian River inlet. I worked for the Corps of Engineers until 1941. Then I went to work for Curtis Bay Ordnance as a pile driving instructor. From there I worked as a civilian for the government at various places. Then in 1944 I went to work for DuPont in Delaware. The job was supposed to be for only the duration of the war. Well it lasted for thirty years and one month, until I retired in 1974.

"I made my first decoys in 1946. Up until 1945 I got my decoys from Bill Heverin. I would furnish him the wood and he would make my decoys. He only made four species; Canvasbacks, Black Ducks, Redheads and Blackheads.

"I got my first decoys from Bill Heverin in 1926. I was 13 years old. My father introduced me to him and told me that he made decoys. Well, I needed decoys and Bill told me to get some wood and he would make me my decoys. I found an old white pine log that had floated down the Susquehanna and ended up back in the marsh. I cut that log up with a cross cut saw and took the wood to him. He made me around 70 decoys out of that log. The decoys cost thirty five cents a piece.

Joseph Evans McKinney paints the eye of a Redhead drake.

Redhead drake by Mr. McKinney.

"After he died I went on to make my own. I just started making decoys because I thought I could make them. I didn't really need them. I still had plenty of decoys. I was still gunning at that time. But we weren't gunning sinkbox. After they stopped sinkbox gunning we bushwhacked. I preferred sinkbox gunning. Ducks look a lot closer to you, but they weren't as close as you thought they were. You had a tendency to jump the gun.

"On one particular hunt we had cut a hole in the ice for the sinkbox. We gunned for three days and killed a total of 220 Canvasbacks. This was back in the late 1920s. We sold them for $6.00 to $7.00 a pair. The ducks were shipped to restaurants in Philadelphia and New York in boxes marked as fresh fish.

"Bill Heverin influenced my style of decoy carving. But not the painting. Back then most of the carvers didn't put any wing paint on Canvasbacks. They were just the basic color, no detail. Bob McGaw was the first one that I know of to put wings on a Canvasback. Sam Barnes' daughter, Florence, did it also. She painted ducks for Sam. My painting is more or less my own style.

"I make the head and body for my decoys out of white pine. I've never owned a machine of my own to make decoys. For a long time I would take the blocks of wood to Madison Mitchell and he would turn the bodies for me. After he stopped making decoys I quit using machine turned bodies.

"For the paints I use all Japan colors.

"Since I don't have a machine the first thing I do is saw the wood with a band saw. Then I chop it with a hatchet. Then I draw knife it and then spoke shave it. After I have chopped a decoy I can draw knife it and spoke shave it in 15 minutes.

"I guess I have made over a thousand decoys in my time. Some were machine-turned and some hand-chopped. I'm partial to the Canvasback, but I've made Redheads, Bluebills, Black Ducks, Coots, Mallards, Blue-winged Teals, Baldpates, and Goldeneyes. I've also made about a dozen swans.

"As time passed I have changed the head style of my decoys. I just saw the duck differently.

"I started gunning when I was 13 years old with my father and brother. My first gun was a 16 gauge single barrel from Sears and Roebuck. The gun cost $6.35. We just gunned off of the point. We would put out a few decoys, but they weren't that important back then. The ducks were more plentiful then and a few decoys would attract them. Some days, if the winds were right, we would pick up as many as 40 decoys that had broken loose from other rigs on the Flats. People just didn't bother to go after them. The Canvasback was considered the number one duck to shoot and then it was the Redhead. The Black Duck was considered a trash duck in those days.

"There wasn't a lot of enforcement of the laws back when I was gunning. The one thing you had to be careful of was to be sure that you didn't go on the Flats before 3:15 in the morning. And you weren't allowed out there on an off day. You were only allowed to gun on Monday, Wednesday and Friday. This was back before they outlawed the sinkbox. The off days for hunting gave the ducks a chance to rest and feed.

"I got arrested one time for killing over the limit. They took my ducks from me and I had to pay a fine of $87.00. The irony of it was I was only three over my limit. At that time the limit was four birds a day. Another time I got a citation for gunning too close to bait in a goose field.

"One of my most memorable hunts was back in 1942. It was the first day of the season. You could not tell the hens from the drake Canvasbacks because they hadn't colored that much. We killed around 97 Canvasbacks and 4 Redheads. We went back the very next day to the exact same spot, bushwhacking, and killed 45 Canvasbacks. This was on the Susquehanna Flats. There was no wind. It was dead calm. On an average there would probably be 25 sinkbox rigs and 50 or so bushwhack rigs.

"I can remember Mr. Heverin some times putting a red eye or a yellow eye in a drake Canvasback. One time I asked him why he did that and he told me when the ducks get that close to the decoy it doesn't make any difference what color eyes they have. I guess he painted them that way due to the lack of paint he may of had at that time."

John H. McKinney
Born: 1889 lived in Chestertown, Kent County, Maryland
Died: 1973

Top, miniature Wood Duck by John H. McKinney.

Full-size Canvasback drake by Mr. McKinney.

Left, dead Canvasback drake decoy. Right, dead Mallard drake decoy by Mr. McKinney.

Flying Canvasback drake decoy by John H. McKinney.

Full-size Mallard drake decoy by John H. McKinney.

John Meredith

"I was born in Toddsville, Maryland on December 5, 1946. I began making decoys out of necessity. Most people could not afford to buy new decoys to gun, so they would find old ones floating on the shores or make their own out of whatever was available.

"I started working as a waterman, then later moved to Still Pond where I became a truck driver. I now makes decoys full time.

"I used to buy a bushel basket of decoys for fifty cents. I'd go to auctions or sales to find them. My dad would tell me 'Boy, you're crazy! You work all week and then go out there to them sales and buy them old decoys. What are you going to do with them?' 'I just want them,' I told him. I had seventy-five or eighty Mitchell's and five or six fish boxes full of Mason's for a total collection of two hundred eighty-five birds. It also included three pair of Ward's which where a dollar apiece in 1959 or 1960. I bought them from my grandfather who had five or six hundred up there. I bought all I could and told him to hang on to the rest while I tried to make another fifteen or twenty dollars during the week.

"Charlie Joiner is my hero and that's all there is to it. He made the best looking decoy I ever saw. His decoys have been a great love of mine even when I didn't know one from another. I only knew his name as Speed Joiner, never knew him as Charlie. It wasn't till '84 that I got to meet him. That was the year I got to make the Green Wing Teal for Ducks Unlimited. Speed was more excited than I was that someone from Kent County was selected to make the bird. He said 'I'll help you to make that bird right, but I don't want you to paint it to look like my paint job.' 'Charlie,' I said, 'when I get done with it, it's not possible for it to look like your paint job.' That teal turned out looking pretty good.

John M. Meredith holds a Ruddy Duck drake. Ruddy Duck hen rests on paint table.

Top left clockwise: full-size Redhead drake, Redhead hen, Red-breasted Merganser drake, Ruddy Duck hen, Ruddy Duck drake and Red-breasted Merganser hen made by John M. Meredith.

"When I was a kid I would use anything I could find to make decoys. From 1962 to 1966 I used cork to make Blackducks and Canada Geese. Now I use Canadian white cedar and Tupelo gum from North Carolina. I used to hand-chop decoys at first, now I use machines a lot. I never did sand the decoys back then, nothing was rounded off, not even the heads. They didn't have to look good to decoy ducks. They got painted with what ever Dad had in the barn, oil or latex paint.

"I probably made two hundred fifty to three hundred decoys as a teenager. Professionally, I have made several thousand. My wife helps by sanding and I have brought my son and daughter into the business also. My wife does the decorative decoys and has won many awards. My son also does decorative and my daughter makes shore birds. People who buy my decoys range from gunners, who use them, to collectors. Lots of professional people buy them.

"My grandfather used to take me gunning when I was eight years old to help feed the family. He let me shoot the 410 gauge. I still have it today. Later on I favored the 12 gauge Browning automatic. We hunted in Fishing Bay, Blackwater River and Transquaking River, all in Dorchester County. Elwood Robinson was my grandfather. Lurman Robinson, Arthur Mills, Shriver Mills and Wilson Mills were all kin. All of these men were watermen.

"We shot Buffle Heads, Hair Heads (Red Breasted Mergansers), Blackducks, Black Heads, and Canvasbacks. So that's what we made decoys for. My grandfather was the overseer of Charles Creek Gunning Club. He got me a job doing whatever there needed to be done, putting out decoys, brushing blinds and calling in ducks for the members. I'm the grandson of a market hunter.

I saw five guys shooting automatics with extended magazines that held 9 to 12 shells each. When they emptied their guns there were ninety Black Ducks dead on the water from one pull down. The sky was almost black with them and there was a hole cut out of the center when they shot. It was awesome. It stunned me. The anticipation of waiting for the shot was great, but when the shooting was done it scared the hell out of you that you had done that. I really can't say I felt bad because we used every bird, nothing was wasted.

"The Canvasback duck is my favorite, because of the way it flew, looked and tasted. My most memorable hunt was with my Uncle Elwood. We killed one hundred fifty eight Canvasbacks in forty five minutes one day on the only water hole open in the ice. In Blackwater, we used to hide in the grass and bushwhack the geese. Even today we eat a lot of wild game like deer, but nothing's killed illegal anymore. We still believe you don't waste anything."

Full-size two headed American Coot by Mr. Mitchell. Design came from Steve "Stevie" Lay. About fifty or sixty were made.

R. Madison Mitchell

"I was born March 11, 1901 in Oakington, Maryland in Harford County. I had nine years of schooling in Havre de Grace and three and a half in Baltimore Business college. In 1918, while going to school, I started working at nights and Sundays for my uncle John O. Mitchell who was a funeral director in Baltimore. He owned the Mitchell Funeral Home there."

"I knew when I was seven years old that I wanted to be a funeral director. I had a great uncle, E. Madison Mitchell, who was not only a funeral director but had a stable of race horses. He used to come up to the farm about every four or five weeks. He would always bring a market basket full of goodies. In that basket he would always have a toy for me. Mister, I thought the sun rose and set on the gentleman. I was named Robert Madison Mitchell, but would never answer to the name Robert. I was booted, put away from the table, and smacked. My mother took me to school and told the teacher, 'You're going to have to call him Madison; he won't answer to Robert.' She said, 'Mrs. Mitchell, it says his first name is Robert and that is what he will be called.' After three or four days she came around to my desk and shook me by my shoulders and said, 'Didn't you hear me call you?' I said, 'No mam, you did not call me. My father is Robert Mitchell. My name is Madison, and it still is today.'

"I got my directors license in 1922. I started my funeral home July 8th at twelve noon, 1924. This year, 1989, on that date I will have been at that one address sixty-five years.

"When I came here some of my friends wanted me to sell life insurance; some wanted me to sell tombstones; and some wanted me to sell real-estate. This was in addition to being a funeral director. I made up my mind that I wanted something I could lay down immediately whenever a call came in to the funeral home. One day, Sam Barnes, who was my cousin, came by and said, 'I helped you paint your funeral home; now I'm behind in making decoys.' I said, 'Cousin Sam, you helped me, now I will help you.' He said, 'What do you know about making decoys?' I said, 'The same thing you did when you started, nothing.' That is how I got started with him.

R. Madison Mitchell finishes painting Canvasback drake. Canvasback hen sits on paint table as Pintail drake and hen hang on wall behind Mr. Mitchell. R. Madison Mitchell was selected as the First Honorary Chairman for the Havre de Grace Decoy Festival in 1982. Complete collections of Mitchell decoys were sold at auction.

Full-size American Coot by Mr. Mitchell.

Top, full-size highneck Canvasback drake. Bottom, full-size Canvasback hen by R. Madison Mitchell.

"It was the last part of July, 1924, when that all took place. He would chop the bodies out and I would spoke shave them. He was one of those old gentlemen that never stopped; he just kept on working. I knew immediately what he was going to ask me to do, and that was to hand sand those two bushels of heads sitting there. I stopped in Bob McGaw's shop one afternoon and told Bob what I wanted and he said 'Help yourself, there is a whole bunch of them over there on the work bench.' It was worn out sanding belts I was looking for. After I left Bob's shop I went to see old Mr. Wertky and told him I wanted him to make me a sander like Bob's. He went with me up to McGaw's shop to look at his sander. We decided to make it so it would run a two inch and a four inch belt. It wasn't two weeks before Sam said, 'You had better get those two bushels of heads and get them sanded.' I asked if I could take them home to work on them. 'I don't care as long as you bring them back tomorrow morning,' he said.

"I had that sanding machine mounted on two by eights up against the inside wash house wall. When it ran it shook the whole building. I could sand out heads on that machine four to one compared to sanding by hand. About a week later he gave me another bushel of heads to do. He said, 'You're not going up to Bob McGaw's are you?' I said, 'No, I'm not going up to Bob McGaw's.' They hated each other like nobody's business. It was just jealousy. When he came up to find me one day he found me sanding those heads on that machine. He said 'You'll have to bring that down to my shop.' 'You'll have to get your own, cousin Sam,' I said. He had one made, but not with two belts, only one belt because he was tight with money.

"I soon learned to head the ducks and most of the other wood working chores. Although I didn't learn to whittle heads too much with Sam. He only lived two more years, then he died in February of 1926. There were already many orders for decoys for that fall. I said to his daughter Florence, who did most of his painting, 'If I get all those ducks made, can we fill those orders?' She said,
'I don't see why not.' I started in immediately to make those ducks, about fourteen hundred in all. I started hunting up lumber. I had to buy wood for the heads; Sam had a few boys up in Pennsylvania that he bought wood from. They would bring wood in return for finished decoys. I call it the barter system. Of all those big upriver decoys I made, only a few paid a nickel for them. The wood came from Pennsylvania bridges, foundries, warehouses, and barns when they tore them down. Anyway, I got the decoys made and primed by the last of July. I went to see Florence at her mother's house to get her to paint them. Her mother said, 'Didn't you hear? Florence got married a month ago and moved to Philadelphia.' I call her on the phone to ask her to come back and paint and she said, 'Madison, I ain't never coming back to Havre de Grace.' And she didn't. I asked all of the piddlers around town if they knew how to paint them, but they didn't know either.

"The major decoy maker then was Bob McGaw, but I didn't go ask him. His father-in-law, Mr. Moore, did most of his painting. I was out front cleaning up one morning when he came by and said, 'How you coming with your paint?' I said,
'Boss, I don't even know where to start.' He said, 'What do ya mean?' I told him that I knew nothing about mixing paint, didn't have any brushes and didn't know what to buy. He said, 'You're in trouble but, I'll tell you what I'll do. I'll come up tomorrow morning and we'll make up a list and I'll tell you where to get 'em.'

"I went to Baltimore to Budeke's paint store on Broadway to buy the paint and brushes. I looked at all that stuff and said to Mr. Budeke,

Top, full-size Ringneck drake. Bottom, full-size Ringneck hen by Mr. Mitchell.

'You had better stop and check that bunch of stuff; it looks like you got a lot of money there.' He had about thirty dollars more added up than I had money to pay him with.' I said, 'Will you take a check?' 'Mr. Mitchell, I don't even know you,' he said. 'I helped on your mother and father's funeral when I worked for my uncle John O. Mitchell. Call him up, I know he'll back me up.' Mr. Budeke said, 'If he's your uncle, I'll take your check.'

"Old Mr. Moore came up and helped me mix the paint and to get started one morning when Bob McGaw saw him. Bob got to the top of the steps and looked at the old gentleman and said, 'What the hell are you doing here?' Mr. Moore said, 'I'm helping Madison get started.' You know, Bob McGaw never spoke to that old man again as long as he lived, and he lived in the same house with Bob McGaw. He never let him paint any more decoys for him either. Mr. Moore said to me one day, 'He did me a favor, now I don't have to paint any more of those damn decoys for him.' He always helped me paint and would never take any money.

"Those fourteen hundred decoys were finished before the first day of gunnin' that year. The average order then was from fifty to a hundred decoys and they sold for a dollar and a half each.

"My first employee was Mr. Ed Way. He used to make a few decoys to pay for coal for his heat in the winter. The old gentleman and I got to talking one day and he said, 'I'll tell what I'll do. I won't make any more decoys, I'll whittle your heads for you for ten cents a piece.' I said, 'That's a deal.'

"I'll never forget the night that Ed Sampson came by my shop and asked for a job. I said, 'You got a job at the proving grounds don't you.' He said, 'Yes, but I need seven pair of shoes and seven overcoats for my children.' I asked him if he knew what a spoke shave and a draw knife were. 'I know what they look like but I don't know how to use them.' 'Do you want to learn to use them?' I asked. 'Yes I do,' he said. 'How much money do you make at the proving grounds?' I asked. 'Eighty-four cents an hour,' he said. 'I can't pay you that,' I told him. 'How much can you pay?' he asked. 'A dollar an hour,' I said. 'I'll take it too,' he said real fast. He was rough at first. I would go over his heads after I finished painting at night so someone could whittle them the next morning. After three weeks no one could touch him.

"I would make decoys in the summer time and paint them toward the fall. In the winter time I would move to the basement of the funeral home and make miniatures. Very little was done after Christmas to April. In 1929 and 1930 I hand chopped all the decoys. I guess there are about fifteen hundred hand chopped decoys out there somewhere but I haven't seen but a few.

"Bob McGaw had the first decoy machine. I had old man Wertky build me a machine to turn decoy bodies. Bob had a different kind of cutter on that machine when he used it. One day one of the teeth flew off and went through the floor about a foot behind him. He finished up those blocks and he never started it up again.

"I bought the machine from him for three hundred and seventy-five dollars. I took it apart and went to Baltimore and had a saw blade fitted where he had those cutters. He saw it and said, 'Aw, you have to ruin everything.' 'It's mine, I paid you for it, and I can do what I want with it,' I said. That was a lot of money, but it would do a lot of work too. I bought Bob's machine and Paul Gibson bought mine. We moved them both the same day.

"In 1934, when the Canvasbacks, Blackheads, and Redheads left here, there were about twelve hen to fifteen drakes. When they came back in the fall there was one hen to twenty one drakes. The ducks

Full-size Black Duck by Mr. Mitchell.

Top, full-size Northern Shoveler drake. Bottom, full-size Northern Shoveler hen by Mr. Mitchell.

Top, full-size Cinnamon Teal drake. Bottom, full-size Cinnamon Teal hen by Mr. Mitchell.

Top, full-size Green-winged Teal drake. Bottom, full-size Green-winged Teal hen by Mr. Mitchell.

Top, full-size Blue-winged Teal drake. Bottom, full-size Blue-winged Teal hen by Mr. Mitchell.

went to Canada and the pot holes dried up. The rains came too late for the little one's to feather out in time to migrate. The hens stayed with the little ones and they froze to death. The rest of the Canvasbacks got up and migrated south. This happened two years straight. That is when Ducks Unlimited started.

"They outlawed the sinkbox then. The people who had those big rigs quit hunting. They sold all those decoys for fifty and seventy five cents a piece. All the new decoys that I had made sat on the shelf. I didn't sell a decoy for two years. A friend of mine who was in the insurance business bought those old decoys by the hundreds. Then he brought them to me for repair. New heads and repainting was all I did for three years. Before the sinkbox was outlawed the limit was one hundred ducks to a boat. It was after 1934 that I started making puddle duck decoys like Mallards.

"I remember when I was about fourteen years old. My sister got married and moved to a farm in Anne Arundel County. That September before school started she convinced my father to let me come spend a week with her. I noticed that every afternoon a dickens of a bunch of doves would come in there to a small pond surrounded by locust trees. I decided I was going to kill me a mess of doves. I asked my brother-in-law what kind of gun I could use. He offered me a double and a single barrel and said, 'With the single you won't shoot so many shells.' I ended up killing twenty-four doves. I went up to the house and my sister said, 'I'll tell you what you do. You pick and clean them and we'll have a dove potpie.' My brother-in-law came up from milkin' and said, 'You didn't come down to the barn and help me milk.' I said, 'I'm still pickin'.' Mister, when I finished cleaning them I knew I would never kill another dove.

"I remember an old fellow by the name of Will Beck that went down outside of the park island and put on a pair of chest waders. He put out about thirty-five decoys and stood in the middle of them. He killed about a dozen ducks on that Saturday afternoon. When Eddie Mauldin came home from the war I got him to go watch Will shoot those ducks one morning. He said, 'That guy is crazy.' The old man had a Sam Barns swan in front of him and he laid his gun on it. I'll never forget it. Ed and I made up our mind that if he could do it we would go out on the flats and do it.

"We built a stool of three hundred geese and Black Ducks and started body booting. Elmer Simpers gunned with us a couple of times and told everyone he started it. I told him Will started it and he knew it. We made oversized full body Swans and built a gun rack on it. I have never seen one of those swans since. I don't know what happened to them.

"I started my own patterns off Daddy Holly's. His pattern was only twelve inches long. I made mine thirteen inches long. Sam Barns' decoys were nowhere near that size. After 1934 we went to making everything, Sprigtails (Pintails), Mallards, Black Ducks, and Canada Geese. You couldn't use live decoys so they needed decoys.

"I wished I had kept records as to how many decoys I've made. I wished I would have kept records, too, of all the big rigs of decoys that were out there on those flats, but I didn't and no one can tell you about it now. I broke the law once or twice but I didn't make a habit of it. I never night gunned or sold a duck, but I have bought a few.

"My uncle called me up one night and said, 'Madison, I've got some friends who would like to have some Canvasbacks. Can you get any?' 'How many do you want?' I asked. 'All you can get,' he said. I

Top, full-size Redhead drake. Bottom, full-size Redhead hen by R. Madison Mitchell.

Top, full-size Pintail drake. Bottom, full-size Pintail hen by R. Madison Mitchell.

Top, full-size American Widgeon (Baldpate) drake. Bottom, full-size American Widgeon (Baldpate) hen by R. Madison Mitchell.

Top, full-size Blackhead drake. Bottom, full-size Blackhead hen by Mr. Mitchell.

Top, full-size cork Bufflehead drake. Bottom, full-size cork Bufflehead hen by Mr. Mitchell.

bought forty pair for five dollars a pair, at about two o'clock in the morning from Henry Keen. He loaded up my car and I headed for Baltimore. I was going up past the American Legion where there was a weigh station for a bus stop. I saw a fellow I recognized standing there, Biff Merker. I said, 'Biff, if you're going to Baltimore I'll take you down.' As soon as he got in he started looking in the back. 'If you get in the back snoopin' around I'll throw your ass out and you'll walk to Baltimore,' I said, kidding. I let him off on Greenmount Avenue and went to my uncles to deliver the ducks. Biff came home before me and what did he do? He looked up Oden King, the Federal Game Warden and told him what he suspected I was doing last night. That evening I stopped in at Bob McGaw's and Oden was there too. He said, 'I came near locking you up this morning.' I said, 'What are you talking about.' 'When you picked up those ducks last night.' 'You're crazy as hell,' I said. 'You ought to know, you took them to Baltimore.' 'The next time you see Biff Merker, you tell that so-and-so the next time he wants to go to Baltimore, he can walk.'

"Once Bobby Wilson and I killed two bags of Black Ducks and about thirty geese while body-booting. I quit gunnin' at 10:30 in the morning. I pulled the big boat into the middle of the decoys, set there and started eating lunch. Bobby raised cane. I said, 'I don't care, you ain't goin' to gun anymore today. You killed too many now. We don't have any iron in the boat to sink the ducks, and if we get caught we'll be in jail for a thousand years.' Bobby just laughed and shook his head. You know, one bag of Black Ducks equals about twenty Black Ducks.

"The last time I gunned was in '68 or '69 with Harry Jobes. He and I had made twenty-five cork Canvasbacks. He was working for himself then. He came up to my shop and wanted me to go gunnin'. Harry always laid out his stool like a horse shoe. He could scull through the center and not touch a thing. In the toe of the shoe is where he would lay out those cork Canvasbacks. He'd swear that those Canvasbacks would swim into those corks and go to sleep. I said, 'You're the biggest liar in Havre de Grace.' Harry Linkinfelter, the mail carrier, was scullin' for us that day. We were setting there watchin' the decoys when some ducks went into those decoys. We scrambled to get in the boat and Harry Linkinfelter said, 'I don't mind scullin' you boys, but I want you to kill somethin'.' I said, 'Where in the dickens are those bunch of ducks? I haven't taken my eyes off them, but I don't see them.' Harry Jobes said, 'They're down in those corks asleep.' Linkinfelter slapped the side of the boat with the oar. When those ducks got about three feet off the water, Joby and I shot into them. Harry was using a pump shotgun. I had a Winchester 97 pump and an automatic. We killed thirteen canvasbacks. I said to Linkinfelter, 'Take me to shore.' 'You've got to take one more scull,' he said. 'I'll be damned if I do. If I get to shore with these I'll be tickled to death.' We got to shore at the park and I got out and walked all through the park lookin' for the game warden. I didn't see anyone I recognized, so I grabbed those ducks and threw them in the back of the old car. Linkinfelter asked me to take a pair of ducks over by his house and hang them on the nail by his back door. I took those ducks over to his house and I flew out of there, and I have never touched a gun since.

"How Joby and "Titbird" Bauer kept from gettin' locked up that fall I'll never know. They gunned the westward and broke the law every darned day. Titbird was comin' in one afternoon and he saw a cripple comin' off Harry Jobes' outfit. He put the shotgun out the window of his boat and shot it. The game warden caught him. He gave Titbird a ticket and Titbird said, 'I don't want that ticket.' The game warden said, 'You had better want it,' and left it on the front of his boat. Titbird left it there and the wind blew it off into the water. He never heard any more about it.

"I sold the decoy shop to Bill Collins in 1979. My funeral business just about doubled that year and I couldn't do both anymore. I kept painting with him up into September of 1985. I never considered selling the business to anyone else. I trained Bill and wanted him to have it. I have always thought a lot of Bill and I still do."

"Jimmy Pierce and a few others tried to figure out how many I made. About one hundred thousand decoys is what they came up with. You know, everyone of those boys who worked here grew up to all be good men. I never had any trouble with any of them. They made as many decoys for themselves as they did for me. There was a lot of mischief in my shop, a lot of great times. There will never be another shop like that."

Full-size Snow Goose by Mr. Mitchell.

Full-size Blue Goose by Mr. Mitchell.

Full-size Canada Goose being painted by Mr. Mitchell.

Pair of full-size Morning Doves by Mr. Mitchell.

Pair of full-size Pigeons by Mr. Mitchell.

Top, cast iron Canvasback hen sinkbox (wing duck) decoy. Bottom, cast iron Canvasback drake sinkbox (wing duck) decoy by R. Madison Mitchell.

Full-size Whistling (Tundra) Swan with keel by M' F. McGaw.

Top, full-size decorative Wood Duck drake. Bottom, full-size decorative Wood Duck hen sleeper by Mr. Mitchell.

Top, full-size decorative Common Goldeneye drake. Bottom, full-size decorative Common Goldeneye hen by Mr. Mitchell.

Top, full-size decorative Northern Shoveler drake. Bottom, full-size decorative Northern Shoveler hen by Mr. Mitchell.

Top, full-size decorative Bufflehead drake. Bottom, full-size decorative Bufflehead hen by Mr. Mitchell.

Top, full-size decorative Pintail hen. Bottom, full-size decorative Pintail drake by Mr. Mitchell.

Top, full-size decorative Blackhead drake. Bottom, full-size decorative Blackhead hen by Mr. Mitchell.

Top, full-size decorative Common Goldeneye drake. Bottom, full-size decorative Common Goldeneye hen by Mr. Mitchell.

Top, full-size decorative Redhead drake sleeper. Bottom, full-size decorative Redhead hen sleeper by Mr. Mitchell.

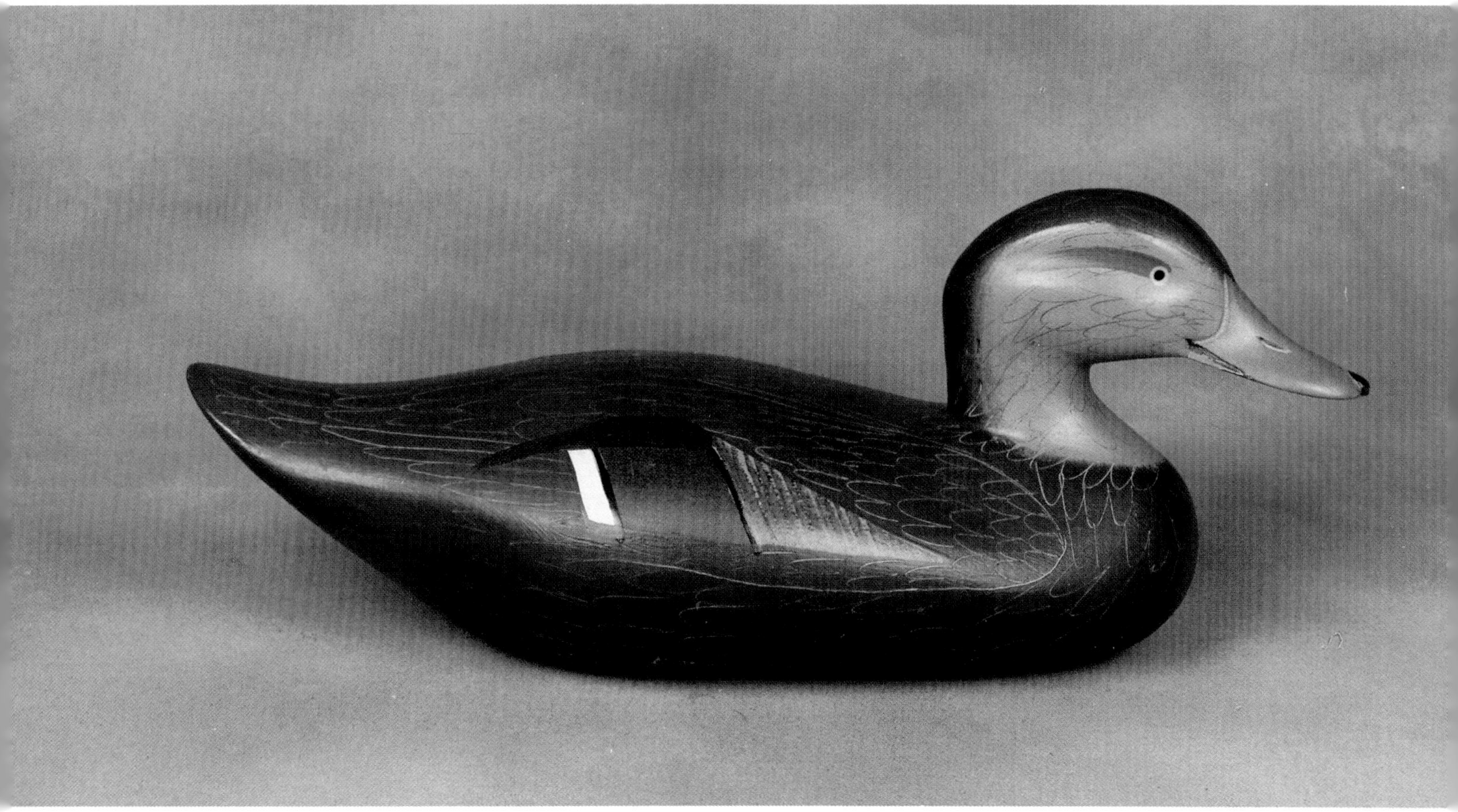

Decorative Black Duck by Mr. Mitchell.

Top, full-size decorative Mallard drake sleeper. Bottom, full-size decorative Mallard hen sleeper by Mr. Mitchell.

Top, full-size decorative American Widgeon (Baldpate) drake. Bottom, full-size decorative American Widgeon (Baldpate) hen by Mr. Mitchell.

Decorative American Coot by Mr. Mitchell.

Top, full-size decorative Canvasback drake sleeper. Bottom, full-size decorative Canvasback hen sleeper by Mr. Mitchell.

Top, full-size decorative Mallard drake. Bottom, full-size decorative Mallard hen by Mr. Mitchell.

Top, full-size decorative Wood Duck drake. Bottom, full-size decorative Wood Duck hen by Mr. Mitchell.

Top, full-size decorative Whistling (Tundra) Swan by Mr. Mitchell.

Top, full-size cork Wood Duck drake. Bottom, full-size cork Wood Duck hen by Mr. Mitchell.

Top, full-size cork Blackhead drake. Bottom, full-size cork Blackhead hen by Mr. Mitchell.

Top, full-size cork Pintail hen. Bottom, full-size cork Pintail drake by Mr. Mitchell.

Top, full-size cork American Widgeon (Baldpate) hen. Bottom, full-size cork American Widgeon (Baldpate) drake by R. Madison Mitchell.

Top, full-size cork Common Goldeneye hen. Bottom, full-size cork Common Goldeneye drake by Mr. Mitchell.

Top, full-size cork Cinnamon Teal drake. Bottom, full-size cork Cinnamon Teal hen by Mr. Mitchell.

Top, full-size cork Green-winged Teal drake. Bottom, full-size cork Green-winged Teal hen by Mr. Mitchell.

Top, full-size cork Blue-winged Teal drake. Bottom, full-size cork Blue-winged Teal hen by Mr. Mitchell.

Top, full-size cork Redhead drake. Bottom, full-size cork Redhead hen by Mr. Mitchell.

Top, full-size cork Canvasback drake. Bottom, full-size cork Canvasback hen by Mr. Mitchell.

Top, full-size cork Mallard drake. Bottom, full-size cork Mallard hen by Mr. Mitchell.

Full-size cork Brant by Mr. Mitchell.

Full-size cork Snow Goose by Mr. Mitchell.

Full-size cork Canada Goose by Mr. Mitchell.

Full-size cork Whistling (Tundra) Swan by Mr. Mitchell.

Full-size cork American Coot by Mr. Mitchell.

Full-size cork Black Duck by Mr. Mitchell.

In 1984, Madison Mitchell watches Bill Collins (right) paint eyes on decoy. Mr. Collins, Bill's father, also watches from left rear.

Full-size Canada Goose Scooter was produced in unknown numbers at Christmas time for childrens gifts.

Canvasback hen and drake cast iron bookends by R. Madison Mitchell.

Hand chopped highneck Canvasback drake. One of the very few that Mr. Mitchell hand chopped. After the sinkbox was outlawed in 1932 all of the highneck decoys were refitted with the shorter heads. This one somehow escaped and was being still being gunned over till the 1970's. It was donated to R. Madison Mitchell for the Havre de Grace Decoy Museum by Mr. Bruce Bartenfelder and family.

Top left clockwise: miniature Mallard hen, miniature Black Duck, miniature Black Duck and miniature Mallard drake made by Mr. Mitchell.

Top, miniature Pintail hen. Bottom, miniature Pintail drake made by Mr. Mitchell.

Pair of miniature Whistling (Tundra) Swans made by R. Madison Mitchell.

Top left clockwise: miniature Redhead hen, miniature American Widgeon (Baldpate) hen, miniature American Widgeon (Baldpate) drake and miniature Redhead drake made by Mr. Mitchell.

Top left clockwise: miniature Canvasback hen, miniature Blackhead hen, miniature Blackhead drake and miniature Canvasback drake made by Mr. Mitchell.

Pair of miniature Canada Geese made by Mr. Mitchell.

R. Madison Mitchell stands next to the decoy lathe on lower level of his shop. It is now in the Havre de Grace Decoy Museum on display along with the rest of his shop.

Mr. Mitchell puts Mallard drake in body vise for repair.

Pair of cast iron Canada Goose head bookends made by Mr. Mitchell.

Full-size Mallard drake lamp made by Mr. Mitchell.

Half and half decoy. This full-size decoy was painted as a Redhead drake on one side and Blackhead drake on the other by R. Madison Mitchell to be used as a paint pattern for William Boyd.

Half and half decoy. This full-size decoy was painted as a Blackhead drake on one side and Blackhead hen on the other by R. Madison Mitchell. It was to be used as a paint pattern for William Boyd.

Madison Mitchell paints wing feathers on one of only fourteen cork Wood Ducks ever made.

Half-size Whistling (Tundra) Swan made by Mr. Mitchell.

Full-size Whistling (Tundra) Swan with straight neck made by R. Madison Mitchell.

Top left clockwise: Historic gathering in 1983 of Charles "Speed" Joiner, R. Madison Mitchell and Lem Ward in the Ward brothers decoy shop in Crisfield, MD. This was the last time they were together while Lem Ward was alive.

Half-size Canada Goose made by Mr. Mitchell.

"Working with the Master" Left to right: James "Jimmy" Ivan Pierce, R. Madison Mitchell, Charles "Speed" Joiner and Charles "Charlie" Bryan.

Ase Owens
Born: 1876 lived in Perryville, Cecil County, Maryland
Died: 1965

Full-size Canvasback hen made by Ase Owens.

Edwin E. Pearson
Born: 1859 lived in Havre de Grace, Harford County, Maryland
Died: 1932

Full-size Canvasback hen made by Edwin E. Pearson.

Full-size Canvasback drake made by Edwin E. Pearson.

Frederick Steiner Pierce

"I was born December 10, 1927. I was born and raised in Havre de Grace. I graduated from high school however there were only eleven grades back then. I have worked the C & P Phone Company as a repairman. I retired in 1986.

"The reason I started to make decoys was because of my brother Jimmy. Back in the forties Jimmy had a shop down on Franklin Street in Havre De Grace where a bunch of us boys would always hang around and helped to make decoys for our own use. I used to go down to Mitchell's a good bit because Jimmy worked there, but I never worked there.

"I did a lot of different things but didn't get serious about decoys until 1974 or '75. I have my own shop today. I have made a lot of miniature and half-size gunning decoys. Shore birds and full size duck decoys are what I'm making now. In all I guess I have made about three or four hundred decoys a year. When I need bodies I go up and use Jimmy's decoy machine, then I bring them down here.

"I don't go for all the different body styles for each species. I have settled on a few and make all of my birds to suit them. I paint the decoys according to what mood I'm in. I have painted some like the Joiner style. Then I'll go back to the Havre de Grace style. My son works with the decoys some, but he works for Jimmy at times.

"I was privileged enough to bushwhack a good bit. Harry Lingenfelter had a metal boat. Harry was a motormac in the Navy during World War Two. We had heard that the Boston Metal Company down in Baltimore had a bunch of life boats from the old Liberty Ships for sale. There were yards full of those boats. We ended up towing several of those boats home to Penns Beach Marina owned by Henry DeLuka. We built a cabin and put a Grey Marine engine on it. These boats were thirty some feet long. After we fixed that thing up we called it the "Iron Chief". Emerson Mitchell, Jimmy Harry, Milford Wyatt and myself took a week off of work and hunted on the flats. It was in November with warm, shirt sleeve weather and a little foggy. There were no birds flying around, or so it seemed. We started sculling the bushwhack boat toward the decoys when we noticed that we didn't have that many decoys in the water. I guess the Canvasbacks could see over top of that fog and went into the decoys unnoticed. I mean we knocked them. We had about fifteen or twenty Canvasbacks. You didn't see any geese down here till they started to grow corn and use mechanical pickers on the shore."

Frederick Steiner Pierce puts the eye on a half-size Green-winged Teal hen. Left to right on table: pair of shore birds, half-size Green-winged Teal drake, miniature Pintail hen and miniature Pintail drake.

Top left clockwise: Full-size Canvasback hen, Full-size Canvasback drake, Shore bird, half-size American Widgeon (Baldpate) drake, half-size American Widgeon (Baldpate) hen and Dove made by Mr. Pierce.

Jimmy Pierce paints Pintail drake. Baldpate drake sits on paint table and Canvasback drake and hen hang behind him.

James "Jimmy" Ivan Pierce

"I was born May 5, 1934 in Havre de Grace, Maryland.

"My full time profession was working for Bell Telephone Company.

"Decoy making was a hobby I picked up hanging around Madison Mitchell's shop. I liked to hunt and fish. If you wanted to hunt you had to make your own decoys, because you couldn't afford to buy them. So, that's what I ended up doing.

"I made my first decoy when I was thirteen years old. I've been making them ever since then. Most of the time I worked for Madison Mitchell until I got married and eventually opened my own shop. When I was working in Madison's shop, Harry Jobes, Tommy Churns, Ed Cloak, Eddie Mauldin, and all the Sampson boys also worked there. Then came Billy McKenney and Bailey Moats and Bob Matthews. Billy Walker used to be the sander.

"Madison Mitchell was the one who influenced my style of decoy making.

"For my gunning birds I like white cedar wood. For the head I like to use pine. Most of the time it was new wood. I use all oil base paints. Very seldom do I use tube paints, just oils out of the quart cans.

"My birds are machine made. I have hand-chopped some just to do it. I would guess I have made about 25,000 birds in my life time. It's really hard to say. You wonder where they all went to.

"My boys work in the shop with me now and I have a couple of fellows who work part-time. David Walker, Bryon Bodt, Tommy Harman, Butch Wagner, and Dan Carson all worked for me at one time and have gone on to making decoys on their own. And Steve Lay, I forgot him. He worked for me for about fifteen years.

"I've made very little changes in my style of decoy carving. I still copy Mitchell's patterns. And I still use his style of painting. I've just gotten a little neater and a little more particular with it because most of them are going for collecting instead of gunning decoys.

"Up until about fifteen years ago all my decoys were sold for hunting. Now it's all for collections. When I first opened my shop I sold my Canvasbacks for $3.00. I don't have any of them left. But, back then, everything was free. The cedar poles were free, the wood was free and a gallon of paint went for $4.00 and I didn't count my labor as anything.

"My one son, Charlie, likes to fool around making decoys, but I don't know if he is going to stay at it. My other son, J. K., doesn't have the interest in it.

"I've hunted over my own decoys. Whatever we were shooting, we had made the decoys.

"I started hunting when I was about twelve or thirteen years old. Myself, Harry Jobes, Jimmy Collins and my brothers, we always shot birds up the river. Then we got our own bush-whacking rig together for out on the Flats. You didn't need too many decoys then. You could take a half dozen to a dozen decoys and throw them out on the cove and kill some ducks all the time. Back then there was a lot of birds around. On the Susquehanna River there was always Canvasbacks you could shoot. Bush-whacking was just about the best sport of all.

"When we bushwhacked, the first thing you had to have was your whacking boat. Usually there was three of us in a gunning rig. Most of the time we had to have between 125-150 Canvasback decoys to gun with. Mostly drakes. Very few hen birds. That's why people collect today. It's very hard to come by a matched pair of birds that were made back then. You just never made that many hens. You just didn't use them for gunning. Now we make everything in pairs because people buy them in pairs.

"The most birds I ever killed was 167 Canvasbacks by myself. We had had an ice storm the night before and everything was icy. The wind had blown down the river and the water was out pretty low. Everything was skim-ice. I walked the shore line along Cat's Cove up to the stop box, but everything was frozen up. I started walking back and by the time I got to Quarry Wharf the ice had started to move. The ducks started flying up the river and I just laid there and shot all day. I had to go back twice to get shot gun shells.

"We did do some outlaw gunning. For that we altered our guns by putting extensions on them so that they would hold nine rounds. Like I said, that was illegal so we never took them out in the day light. This was for night gunning. You really didn't need to see the ducks because your eyes would adjust to the dark. But the irony of it was that you knew where the ducks were at. You watched where the ducks were going in the evenings. Where they were bedding down. If they were on celery beds or whatever, that's where you went. People don't realize it but back then corn for carp hauls was big business around here. Years ago they used to put, I'm talking about the commercial fishermen, tons of corn all out in different spots for carp and catfish. When they did that the ducks would get on those corn hulls. This was all seasons. January, spring and early fall of the year. You got to remember that catfish was the big industry around here then. There were plenty of catfish. They used to haul and put them in live boxes and take them to the fish house. I didn't feel bad about outlaw gunning because at that time there was an abundance of ducks here. We never thought we were hurting them. They weren't going to waste. They were going for food.

"It used to be a Federal law that you only gunned Canvasbacks on Monday, Wednesday and Friday. Later they included a Saturday. Even if you went out night gunning the gunners respected that day when you weren't supposed to be gunning and they didn't want to see anybody out there. They helped police themselves. It wasn't that there was a shortage of ducks or that the gunner killed all the ducks. We had taken their environment away and we took their habitat away. Once the celery beds were gone around here there began to be less and less ducks every year. Up in Canada they were taking their nesting grounds away from them. It was something against the birds all the time.

"When we would go to Mitchell's shop in the evening we all had khaki pants that we painted in. One night I had on a brand new pair of khakis on, so I changed into my painting pants. Well, when Jobes came in he put my brand new pair of pants on thinking they were his, I suppose. Jobes was bending over and I thought, now look at that, he's got a brand new pair of pants on. So I painted a bulls eye on the seat. Come to find out I had painted my own pants."

Left clockwise: full-size Bufflehead hen, Bufflehead drake and American Widgeon (Baldpate) made by Mr. Pierce.

Leonard E. Pryor
Born: 1876 lived in Elkton, Cecil County, Maryland
Died: 1967

Full-size Canvasback drake considered to be style one made by Leonard E. Pryor.

Full-size Canvasback drake sleeper considered to be style two made by Mr. Pryor.

Full-size Canvasback drake considered to be style three made by Mr. Pryor.

Allen Purner paints wing bar on Blue-winged Teal. Dead Canvasback drake decoy lays on wooden shotshell box in background. Wood Duck drake sits on table in front.

Allen Purner

"I was born January 31, 1921 in Cecil County, the town of North East, Maryland. I worked several different jobs in my time but most of it was for the government. After World War Two was when I started to make decoys for myself to gun over. Later it became lucrative because of the interest in decoys. It turned into a business in 1964. The decoys were not sold for gunning but for collecting. When collecting old fishing gear came to be I started making fish decoys which have sold very well.

"I used to live in 1929 or '30 next to Will Heverin and Scott Jackson who were decoy makers. I had a dog back then that spent as much time with Mr. Heverin as it did me. Heverin's decoys looked and floated the best, compared to the other makers in my estimation. Will Heverin, Scott Jackson and Johnny B. Graham were considered the Charlestown style decoys. What I liked about them was they looked good, wound and off wound good. Instead of hitting you in the mouth with the weights, the weight would go off smooth into the water. The ballast weight was a long rectangular strap weight that went up beyond the curve of the bottom. They were also splayed out so the line would not catch on the bottom. The Bob McGaw weight was the very best in design.

"I liked the Havre de Grace style of wing feathers, the McGaw tail, the primary triangle he used for part of the paint style. A highlight of white paint is put in the eye at two o'clock. The head and the rest of the body I paint to suit myself. The Japan oil colors dry fast and I blend them to get the colors the way I see them.

"The woods I prefer to use are white pine, empress palonia and white western cedar. I use hand chopped decoys and machine run bodies, depending on the species I'm making. Jim Pierce turns the bodies for me. Sometimes I change it a lot with the draw knife to suit my own idea.

Top, Blue-winged Teal drake. Bottom, Blue-winged Teal hen made by Mr. Purner.

View of Mr. Purner's work shop.

"As far as the amount of decoys I have made since I started, it would be twelve hundred to eighteen hundred. This covers all types of decoys. It would be nice to keep a book with what you made, but you never think of that when your doing it. The dead duck decoys were first made by me as far as I know.

"My grandfather was a great gunner, county commissioner and gentleman farmer. When I was about six years old he took me out and let me shoot a shotgun. I bushwhacked in the North East River and the Flats. My sons and I also body-booted on the flats. Bushwhacking was the most sport as far as I'm concerned. I consider myself as a conservationist today. However when I was young, I was like most other gunners in taking an illegal limit from time to time.

"My most memorable hunt was when we couldn't bushwhack because the river was froze up. There was a raft of Canvasbacks in a small hole in the river that they had managed to keep open by diving and splashing about. We made a small opening in the ice near the shore. We put twelve decoys in the hole and the wind was from the north east. It was a good thing it was or they would have heard us uptown shooting. We killed fifty-one Canvasbacks over the course of the day, however, hunters would leave and more would get in the blind. There were a total of twelve hunters to divide up the fifty one birds. We were in violation of the law but not that much. The Canvasback was the most succulent duck to eat when he was feeding on the wild celery on the flats. Bob Litzenberg and I gunned the marshes in a wooden canoe for rail birds. We could kill more in the canoe in one day then most guys could in a season."

Left, dead blue-winged Teal drake decoy. Right, dead Canvasback drake decoy made by Mr. Purner.

An Old Decoy
by
Allen Purner

My time began some years ago, from some sundry piece of wood-As time has passed I've born the wear and tear of use though you'd hardly think I should.
A string hastily tied about my neck wearily trailing some rough and playful boy-I longed to be upon the bay to work, not serving as a misused toy.
I've laid in old sheds, barns or lofts forgotten or stranded on some lonely stretch of shore-to be found in time by some hard put friend and dressed royally again, just as before.
Years have passed since some agile hand did weld my form to bring my prototype to doom-In time to come like as not I will grace some collector's room.
Though only wood and paint to those who have never known what our part could play-the many hours of sport for men and boys, a spanking wind, a whir of wings high above the bay.
Those times have all but passed, but I linger on to warm the hearts of old, slowed by age and time to grace a niche in some warm and knowing heart while the world another trend of sport will find.

Linda Robinson

"I was born August 15, 1948. I graduated from high school and have some college, but not a degree.

"I started making shore bird decoys about three years ago. I started making decoys because I was around them all the time. My husband, Dick, is a carver and I also like working with wood.

"I learned the shore bird making from Jimmy Pierce. He influenced my style and to some degree the painting. Actually my painting is a mix of everybody's to where I came up with my own.

"The wood I mostly use is Jelutong. That is a wood that is imported from Malaysia. I like to use that because it is real easy to carve.

"For my paints I use oils. Not tube, but Japan colors.

"The birds are not machine turned. I use a band saw, draw knife, and carving knives.

"I would guess that I have made about two or three hundred decoys. My husband Dick helps me with the shore birds and I help him with the ducks. I run the lathe for Dick and generally sand most of the small bodies after they come off of the lathe. I've been doing this for about two or three years now. Ever since we got our lathe. I also help Dick putty, prime, and put the color on.

"Our son is also learning the decoy making trade. He is more into the ducks, because he likes to hunt."

Linda Robinson.

Top left clockwise: Plover, Plover, Plover and Spotted Sandpiper made by Linda Robinson.

Dick Robinson paints a half-size Canvasback hen. Half-size Canvasback drake sits on table.

Richard Marshall Robinson

"I was born February 10, 1945 in Fountain Green, Maryland.

"My full-time profession is as an employee for Harford County Department of Public Works. I work in traffic and transportation.

"When I first started making decoys I went to Jimmy Pierce. He was the one that got me going and taught me what I know. Bob Litzenberg, Madison Mitchell and Charlie Bryan have influenced my decoy making also.

"For the woods I use pine, cedar, bass wood and jelutong. For the paints I use Japan colors.

"I really have no idea how many decoys I have made. Probably around 2,000 birds. Mainly miniatures. I haven't made that many full-sized gunning birds.

"About twelve years ago I started waterfowl hunting on the Eastern Shore. We did a little goose and duck hunting. In fact I just purchased some property down below Cambridge to do some duck hunting."

"My favorite species of duck to eat is the Canvasback. I have not hunted them. Not in my time. Another of my favorites would be the Black Duck.

"One particular hunt that comes to mind was several years ago down in Galena. We shot our limit early on and the fellow that was with me took pictures for the rest of the morning. But, I just enjoy hunting, being outside with my friends, and if I get anything, well, that's a bonus. I love watching the birds come in, sit with the decoys, swim around and fly out. It really doesn't whether I shoot the gun or not, I just like watching the birds."

Left front clockwise: full-size Redhead hen, full-size Canvasback drake, half-size Whistling (Tundra) Swan, full-size Canvasback hen and full-size Redhead drake made by Mr. Robinson.

Robert Lee "Bozy" Robinson, Sr.
Born: 1900 lived in Chestertown, Kent County, Maryland
Died: 1968

In front of basket, Redhead drake. Left clockwise in basket: Canvasback hen, Canvasback drake and Blackhead drake made by Robert "Bozy" Lee Robinson Sr.

Edward "Ed" Sampson whittles on half-size duck decoy.

Edward "Ed" Sampson

"I was born August 3, 1902 in Havre de Grace, Maryland right near Rock Run Church. I went to a country school and I only went through the seventh grade.

"I worked anywhere I could make a nickel. I started out working on a farm. Then I worked five years in an ice cream store in Port Deposit. I drove truck five years for a laundry, thirteen years for a bakery and I worked twenty five years as a carpenter at the Aberdeen Proving Ground.

"I started making decoy heads, in September, 1945, at Madison Mitchell's. I was only working part-time at the Proving Grounds and when you're putting seven kids through school you'll do anything. Carpentry was always my main thing. If I couldn't get a job as a carpenter I'd do any thing. I had to make money.

"Madison had to teach me everything. The first thing he had me do when I started down there was make duck heads. I'd throw 'em on the band saw, draw knife 'em and the next guy would whittle 'em and finish 'em up. That's where I started out at Madison's. I did most everything but painting 'em. I never painted because I never had time. I was doing all the other stuff.

"I haven't stopped making decoys. Still am making 'em. I haven't retired, I'm just tired. Still don't paint decoys. My buddy, 'Titbird' Bauer, does all my painting. When he quits painting 'em, that's when I quit making 'em.

"Madison taught me his style of carving. All my patterns are like Mitchell's, except my little swan pattern. I built this little old machine myself out of scrap parts and things. I took the pattern down to Mitchell's and showed him it and he liked it better'n his. I'll be damned if he didn't make a pattern off it. That's the only thing I ever done that was better'n his.

Top, half-size Mallard drake. Bottom, half-size Mallard hen made by Ed Sampson.

Pair of miniature Whistling (Tundra) Swans made by Mr. Sampson.

"Today I mostly use white pine wood or bass wood or old telephone poles for my carving.

"Most of my birds are miniatures and half-size. I've only hand-chopped about two or three birds. My bodies are all turned, that is the miniatures.

"I used to make a lot of the little ones, but I've slowed up a hell of a lot. Right now I've got six to ten orders I've got to make sometime, but I don't know when. When I feel like sitting my ass down to do them, I will.

"One of the people I helped get started was Pat Vincenti. He's still got a head vise that I made for him.

"Years ago I used to rabbit and squirrel hunt. I had a beagle and his name was Jack. He was a good dog. The only problem with him was if he got in a corn field he would hunt field mice instead of rabbits.

"I never duck hunted. Never shot at a duck in my life. I love to eat 'em though. Just as soon as have a Black Duck or a Green Head Mallard as a Canvasback. They are just as good.

"My cousin and I used to hunt together a lot.

"One time I was down at Madison's on a Saturday. We had worked together for about three hours. My son, Billy, was working there also at the time. I was making heads or something when Madison went upstairs. He always kept the bodies up there. He started down the steps with a basket full of 'em and something happened, I don't know what, but down the steps came that whole damn basket of duck bodies. Billy, my son, was standing there working. He looked at them bodies all over the floor and asked if that was all we had coming down the steps. He never missed a beat in his work. Never even offered to help Madison pick 'em up either.

"Ed Cloak, Eddie Mulden, and Willard Duvall, the older carvers, was working at Mitchell's when I was there. So many people worked in there. A lot of the younger ones too, 'Speed' Joiner, Jimmy Pierce, and Capt'n Jobes. I enjoyed all them fellows. We got along just fine. One day there was seven or eight of us in Mitchell's shop and we put together 450-460 ducks that day. One or two guys fitting heads on, one or two nailing them on, and one or two sitting there puttying them and a man over at the sanding machine sanding them as fast as they could nail the heads on.

"Everybody was pretty careful. No accidents. Everybody that cuts a duck head, if he don't cut his fingers once in a while, ain't no damn whittler. You got to cut your fingers once in a while just to make you be careful.

"All three of my sons Bill, Jimmy and Sammy worked at Mitchell's at one time or another. Bill used to do painting. Damn if he didn't get damn near as good as Madison Mitchell. Sammy worked there when he was so small they had to take a Coca-Cola box for him to reach the bench."

Allen Wyane Schauber holds one his Green-winged Teals.

ALLAN WAYNE SCHAUBER

"I was born February 2,1957 in Chestertown, Md.

"I finished high school at Kent County High School. I also took some courses through the Maryland Fire and Rescue Institute, which is also part of the University of Maryland. My full time profession is as a fire fighter at Aberdeen Proving Ground.

"I used to watch my father when I was about fifteen years old making decoys out in the back yard. We always went hunting together. I guess you could say that he influenced me."

"My dad and Charlie Joiner, you could say, were the ones who influenced my style and painting. Not trying to copy either one of them, but taking tidbits from this one and that one, and still trying to come up with a style that was my own.

"The types of wood that I prefer to use are bass wood, pine and, occasionally, white cedar.

"I use artist's oil for my paints. All tube paints. You can't get the colors with acrylics.

"I work in my dad's shop. It's all done with draw knifes, belt sander, hand knifes made by Bob Lominack. He makes all my knifes. The miniatures and full size birds, Black Ducks, Blue Wing Teals are turned bodies. Everything else is hand made. Dick Robinson turns the bodies for me.

"At this point in my life I would say I have made about 150 full-sized birds. Probably about 500-600 miniature decoys.

"I don't employee anybody. I do everything myself. I guess it's kind of like my dad and Charlie Joiner. You do your own thing your self.

"I can see where I try to put a little better detail and I think I have changed my style of painting. It's going to be a lot more like Charlie's than I was painting before.

"I started hunting when I was about ten years old with my dad down in Rock Hall. All water fowl. I have shot the Canvasback, but it has been a long time. I didn't hunt at all in 1988. It's just getting too expensive.

"The most memorable hunt for me happened in 1987. It was the last day of the season on a Friday morning. I came home from work and my dad and I left the house about 8:30 to 9:00, and we were back by 12:00. It was just a Blue Bird day; a beautiful day. We had singles and pairs coming in and we just took our time and got our limit. Talked about the good times and the bad times in the past hunting.

"My favorite species of live ducks are Canvasbacks and Baldpates. I really like Baldpates. I've never made one, but I just think they are pretty. My favorite ones to carve are Canada Goose and Black Ducks.

"I do own a hunting dog. A Yellow Labrador who's two years old. I've just never had the chance to take him hunting."

"When I was about twelve or thirteen years old, my dad and my cousin and myself were hunting down on Jungle Beach, which is down at the end of Still Pond Neck. We needed one Canvasback. I had a single barrel 410. So my dad said 'Here comes a bunch of ducks.' He told me to get ready to shoot. He said 'Pick out a duck, just one duck and you shoot, we won't. Make sure that you get it.' I stood up and shot my duck. Well, everybody else around me started shooting. Since I only had a single barrel gun I didn't shoot any more. Come to find out I had killed a Ringed-neck duck, my dad killed a pair of Golden Eyes and my cousin killed a Bufflehead. Everything else, as far as we know, was Canvasbacks. Out of the whole toll of birds there was only the four that weren't Canvasbacks. We needed the one Canvasback for our limit and we never shot any.

Left front clockwise: Full-size Green-winged Teal drake, Mallard drake, Canvasback drake, Mallard hen and Green-winged Teal hen made by Mr. Schauber.

William "Bill" Arthur Schauber

"I was born February 5, 1938 in Still Pond, Maryland. After attending high school in Chestertown, Maryland I then took some forestry courses in western Maryland. For a while I worked for the State. Right now I'm grounds keeper for the mental health hospital in Chestertown.

"The first bird I made was in 1966. My brother, Eddie, Johnny Curlett, myself and a couple of other fellows were going hunting and we needed some decoys. We went to see Charlie to see if we could buy a couple dozen Canvasbacks. He didn't have any. But he took us into his shop and showed us how to make a flat bottom decoy. My brother Eddie and I ended up making 85 birds in five days. We killed about 250 ducks that year over that bunch of birds. I still have a couple of them.

"I asked Charlie to make me a decorative Canvasback. Charlie said, 'Bill, you can't afford it.' That was the truth too. He was selling them for $15.00 and I offered to give him a dollar a week. He asked me, 'Why don't you make one for yourself?' He gave me a block of wood and lent me a knife. That's all it took. I began from there.

"Charlie Joiner was my influence in my style and also my painting. I still have the patterns that he gave me. I have made some changes along the way so that I don't use a pattern of his. I did it more out of respect for him. I want my birds to resemble his, but not be identical. Now when I make a bird I make a whole new pattern.

"Primarily I use sugar pine wood. I also use a little bit of bass wood. For the painting I use artists oils.

"I have made a gunning style bird, but I don't think any of them have hit the water. They are round-bottomed and some even have keels.

"All my decoys are hand-made. I did make six or eight birds that were turned bodies that I got from Charlie. I don't like making round-bottomed turned birds and I don't have any intention of ever making them again. It was something I had to see if I could do.

"My oldest son, Allan, helped me for a while. Then he started making birds for himself. He would set and watch me. I'm right-handed and he is left-handed so anything I tried to show him was totally backwards. So, basically, Allan taught himself.

"I guess I have made about 800 miniatures and probably, in the last five years, about a couple hundred a year of the full size decoys.

"I used to teach a class in adult education on decoy making. I started out with 31 students and 26 finished their birds. At the end of the year we had a little get together and put all the birds on a display table to be judged. My bird didn't win. One of my students won. Their birds came out just beautiful. Their painting and carving was outstanding. But, none of them has ever made a decoy since then. It was something they wanted to do just once.

"For my style of decoys, I have four or five pictures that I look at. I don't particularly like to copy nature as far as the bird goes. I don't see the two to be the same. To me if it looks absolutely like a goose or a duck you might as well have a stuffed bird. Decoy carving is a work of art. Some of them can be down right ugly but it is still a work of art.

"My customers are all collectors. Come to think of it I did make one rig of decoys for a man in New Jersey. They were over-sized Black Ducks and Mallards. This was around 1974. I happened to meet the gentleman not too long ago and he told me he was still gunning over them.

"As a boy I hunted small game. I also used to sneak out in the field if the geese landed. I would go cut a cedar bush and walk behind it until I would get close enough to shoot them. But the first duck hunting I did was after I was grown. We went goose hunting on the Chesapeake Bay. We had a rig of Canvasbacks and we had a ball. I also guided for Dick Manning for about four or five years for the goose hunters.

"He would have his hunting parties meet him at a local coffee shop before daylight and introduce them to their guide for the day. We got out in the field and got set up. While we were waiting for the geese to start flying I asked them if they wanted me to hunt with them or just call the geese. They told me to just call the geese and they would do the shooting. We had about 5 tolls of geese and they killed one goose.

William "Bill" Arthur Schauber spoke shaves a Pintail body. Pair of finished Wood Ducks sit on work bench.

Mr. Schauber displays a one of a kind decorative Whistling (Tundra) Swan he has hollowed out.

They were some of the worse shots I had ever laid eyes on. Around ten that morning the geese stopped flying so I left for lunch and asked them if they wanted to go along. They said no, there was something they had to do. When I came back I saw that they had set every decoy like little soldiers with an ear of corn in front of each one. It was about 150 silhouettes all lined up in rows. I almost had a heart attack. If the game warden had seen that, we would all still be in jail. I reset the decoys and made them pick up the corn. By the time I got everything straightened out it was about four in the afternoon. Around that time a flight of geese came up the river. I called to them and they headed right for the decoys. The fellows emptied their guns and only killed the one goose. I managed to kill three while they were shooting and they never knew I had even shot my gun. Those two guys were the funniest thing I have ever seen. That is one hunt I will never forget.

"My favorite species of duck for hunting was the Canvasback. I enjoyed eating them too. The next best for eating is the Wood Duck. To me it tastes almost like the Canvasback.

"The best time I ever had shooting was down in Bristol, Virginia right on the Tennessee border hunting Wood Ducks. I've been going down there almost every year since 1972. You jump shoot them. You walk along the woods right next to the stream and they jump up like Quail right under your feet. You can use decoys if you don't like to walk, but you don't need them."

Left front clockwise: full-size Northern Shoveler hen, American Widgeon (Baldpate) drake, Pintail hen, Pintail drake, American Widgeon (Baldpate) hen and Northern Shoveler drake made by Bill Schauber.

George Clifton "Cliff" Simms

"I was born October 12, 1903 in Rock Hall, Maryland. Only went as far as the sixth grade in school. I had to quit because I had to work. I worked on a farm and on the water.

"After a while I went to work in a ship yard in Pennsylvania. Then I went to the ship yard in Baltimore. I tried that for a while but I didn't think much of it. Then I met a fellow who had race horses and I went to work for him exercising horses. We started out at Pimlico Race Track, then we went to Canada. From there we went to Ohio. This was back in 1921. I came back to Rock Hall and got to helping a friend of mine who had a barber shop. I learned the trade and when my friend moved away he left me the shop. I've been in business for myself since 1927. Been cutting hair ever since.

"I was about 36 years old when I started making decoys. We needed them to hunt with and we didn't have the money to buy them. So we started making our own. If I would have had the money to buy a decoy back then it would have been a John Glen decoy. I'm not sure of the price but I think it was around a $1.50. Also as a hobby I had a wood work shop. So I just started making my own decoys. They were all hand-chopped. I didn't even have a band saw to saw them out with.

"I took little bits and pieces of Jess Urie and John Glen's style and came up with my own way of carving. As far as the painting goes we just went with trial and error until I came up with what I wanted.

"Back then we used any kind of wood we could find just so long as it wouldn't sink. The same goes for the paints. We would use house paint or anything we could get a hold of. Of course it was all oil paint.

"Before I got my band saw we would use a little saw for the heads and then whittle them with a knife. The bodies we chopped out with a hatchet, put it in a vise and use a rasp and sand paper to get it down.

George Clifton "Cliff" Simms holds Canvasback drake made in 1989.

Full-size Redhead drake made by Cliff Simms.

Then we put the heads on with a 20 pound nail, right down through the head and then paint it.

"I guess I have made between five hundred and a thousand gunning decoys.

"I used to guide for the gun club I belonged to. I would shoot for the sport too. Sometimes somebody had to kill them. I can recall guiding for former Governor Mandell.

"I started hunting ducks when I was about 12 years old. My favorite species of duck would be the Black Duck. I could eat them every day of the week and not get tired of it. Whereas, the Canvasback sort of had a wild taste to it and I would sort of get a little tired of it.

"I've owned about a dozen bird-dogs in my life. They were all Irish Setters, except for one Pointer. I really enjoy hunting up-land game.

"I gunned a long while and had so many hunting trips it's sort of hard to try and single out one particular one. I used to own Wind Mill Point and I had my booby blind there. I remember one day there was about two or three of us in the booby blind. The wind was blowing and we figured we were going to get some shooting. I sent one of the boys that was with me to the blind on shore where Jess Urie and his son Roger were hunting. I asked them to come out and gun with us. Roger got so excited that he stepped overboard and had to go home and change his clothes. We got some pretty good shooting in that day.

"I quit gunning about seven or eight years ago. I don't really know why I lost interest in it. I guess I just got tired of killing the birds. I've done my share in my life time."

Full-size Canvasback hen made by Mr. Simms.

Captain Jess Urie
Born: 1901 lived in Rock Hall, Kent County, Maryland
Died: 1978

Full-size Canvasback drake made by Captain Jess Urie.

Full-size American Coot made by Captain Urie.

Top, full-size Redhead drake. Bottom, full-size Redhead hen made by Captain Urie.

Roger Urie

"I was born November 9, 1932 in Rock Hall, in the same house I live in today. Our next door neighbor was John Glen who made decoys. In 1945 he needed someone to take over the decoy painting end of his business. That is when I got involved. My dad (Capt. Jess Urie) helped make bodies and heads. I painted under our old Mulberry tree in the back yard. The woodwork was done in our small shop before Dad and me built the larger shop in 1950.

"From 1945 to 1953 we made gunning decoys and all the bodies were hand-chopped. Between 1955 to 1957 I built a decoy machine and sander. We made gunning decoys by machine and stick-ups (goose silhouettes) till 1967. Dad realized the decline in live ducks, therefore he knew there would be a decline in new decoys. From 1967 to 1978 we made stick-ups and miniature decoys. After Dad passed away in 1978, I made only miniature decoys till the present day.

"Dad and I both used Mr. Glen's patterns for a year or so until I designed our own in 1947. Mr. Glen taught me his paint style, and how to mix colors after school. I then taught dad to do the same before I went in the Army.

"Our bodies were made of cedar phone poles, old white pine torn out of buildings, new white pine and bass wood in later years. The first decoys (geese floaters) were made from balsa wood life rafts. Mom would help sand and bolt the staff on the stick ups. In all, I would say we made several thousand full body duck decoys, hundreds of stick ups and thousands of miniature duck, goose and swan decoys.

"Decoys were sold to hunters and sports fishermen that passed though the area. Senator Lloyd Weicker visited our shop in 1971-1972. A pair of Canvasbacks were sent to the Prime Minister of Australia, I remember that the postage was $17.03. Tex Ritter, Vice President of North American Aviation bought some decoys for the crew of Apollo 7. Keep in mind that all decoys were signed by Dad until his death in 1978.

"Hunting was something you grew up with and looked forward to, living on the bay. Dad and I gunned on a small island outside of Rock Hall harbor from 1945 to 1950. We hunted a couple of times with our friend Cliff Simms. We owned several great Chesapeake Bay retrievers over the years. If the duck dove under the water, the dog would follow till he got him.

"The hunt I remember most was the day Glenny Thomas and I were gunning across from the White Horse Point in Swan Creek. Jack Middleton and Dad where in the hedge row at the edge of the water hole, about 500 feet behind us. It was a foggy, misty day and the air was raw. Glenny and I shot our gun barrels hot at Canvasbacks. Dad and Jack bagged Baldpates in the field. What I'll never forget was, I had built a small fire in the blind out of empty shot gun shells. It was burning good and clean. From the roof of the blind we had a canvas cover that was rolled down for the weather. Everything was going fine. While we were getting warm Glenny had picked the feathers off a pigeon he had shot and threw the feathers in the fire. The only thing that comes to mind is the song 'Smoke gets in your eyes.'

"Dad and Jack joined us later for lunch. We had hot dogs in the usual long buns. Dad was smoking one of his cigars that day, which he placed on the edge of the blind on one of the wooden shelves that holds gun shells. We had just handed him a hot dog in a bun when a flight on Canvasbacks started to look us over. Dad quickly put his hot dog down next to his cigar and the dog rolled out of the bun. As you know ducks sometimes make more than one pass at the decoys before going wide and come back tolling. You never know for sure if they will come back. So you relax and go back to what you were doing before all the excitement. Dad picked up without looking, what he thought was the hot dog and placed it back in the bun. At the same time the cans darted back into the decoys. Glenny and I were just about ready to pull the trigger, when all the sudden we heard this awful noise. We looked around and saw Capt. Jess spitting out a mouth full of bun and cigar, half way to the decoys. Glenny and I never got a shot off from laughing so hard. Come to think of it that was the same day some customers got him to sign a pair of miniatures ducks and he signed Capt. Baldpate on one of them. It just wasn't his day."

Captain Roger Urie works on miniature Common Goldeneye drake. Behind him can be seen many varieties of miniature decoys. Roger was selected as Honorary Chairman for the Havre de Grace Decoy Festival in May of 1990. Captain Urie's collection of miniatures and full-size decoys was sold at auction during the show.

Captain Urie holds the first full-size Canvasback drake he has made since 1978. Rogers full-size collection was be sold at auction at the 1990 Havre de Grace Decoy Festival in May of 1990.

Captain Urie is standing next to part of the many bushel baskets of his finished miniature decoys made in 1989.

Previous page:
Miniature decoys of Captain Roger Urie made in 1989.

Patrick "Pat" S. Vincenti

"I was born May 21, 1954 in Bayonne, New Jersey. When I was one year old my family moved to Havre de Grace.

"I graduated from Havre de Grace High School in 1972. After high school I went on to become a baker. I did that until 1986. It was then that I started making decoys full time. My wife Jeannie helped me off and on prior to my doing decoy carving full time. When we went full time she quit her job to do decoy carving with me.

"I started making decoys because I couldn't afford to buy them to hunt over. We started out making silhouettes. I guess I was about 15-16 years old at the time. We made decoys in shop class in school. We drew our first patterns off silhouettes. My first round bottom gunning birds were off Madison Mitchell's patterns. In school in wood shop class we would make lamps and then I would take it to Mr. Mitchell's, and what ever kind of duck he would have left I would buy to put on our lamps. This was back in the late 60's or early 70's. From about 1970-71 I started getting involved in working decoys for my own use.

"Around 1974 I used to hang around at Jimmy Pierce's house quite a bit and some over at Mr. Mitchell's. I got to helping them in the shop sweeping the floor, pulling nails out in the yard, whatever had to be done. Then gradually I started learning the different phases of decoy making. At first every decoy I made was at their expense. They wouldn't charge anything for the wood or the heads or bodies. I believe they were just glad to see somebody young doing the trade. I still have some of the first Mallards I ever painted.

"In 1979 I opened my own shop. I started out with a 12′ x 20′ shed. It didn't have anything in it but a bench and a band saw. I still turned my bodies down at Mr. Gibson's or Mr. Mitchell's. Before 1979 Ed Sampson made all my duck heads, every one of them. I would cut them out on a band saw and sand them, but I never whittled a one. I

Patrick "Pat" S. Vincenti and his wife and partner, Jeannie, display full-size Canvasback drake. Redhead drake sleeper is laying on table.

Sign on the outside of Pat's shop was painted by artist Paul Shertz.

didn't know how to whittle a head. I guess I would have to say that Madison Mitchell had the biggest influence on my learning how. I first started painting my own ducks in 1979. In 1980 I asked "Titbird" to give me a hand on a bunch of Black Ducks. He helped me paint every duck I made from 1980 to about 1983. He did it willingly. He never charged me a penny. Every time I had a batch of ducks to paint, he came. All I had to do was pick up the phone and call him. At that time he was not only painting for himself but also Harry Jobes. From about 1983 on I did the whole decoy myself.

"I would have to say my style of decoys is a combination of all the older fellows. You take one thing from one and something from another, brought it home, started doing it. Basically, from there I came up with my own style. Like my painting; I think I paint very differently from all the rest. A lot of people say it is very close to Mr. Mitchell's way of painting. But, to me, it is totally different.

"For the bodies of my decoys I use white pine or cedar. The heads are all about 98% bass woods.

"I have always used oil based paints. Even the flat looking ones were an oil based paint. Then, over the years as the decoy went from a 'working' to a 'collecting' duck, I felt you had to change the look to make it more appealing to the buyer. Not to the duck hunter, but to the collector. Probably 60% of them are women. When a woman walks into your shop and picks up a duck and it's all chalky and scratchy feeling, she doesn't like it. So we changed the paints to go with the flow.

"I had a band saw when I started my shop. Ed Sampson made me a head vise and Paul Gibson made me a body vise. I still have them today and still use them. Bill Collins made my first draw knife and my first whittling knife. I still have them along with about 15 draw knives and 20 whittling knives. My first lathe was a home-made job I bought in about 1982. A boy from Delaware, Warren Cavender, sold it to me. I made some handmade cork decoys. They were sawed out by the band saw and shaped by hand with a rasp. I never made a hand-chopped duck. But all of my swans, up until about 1988, were all hand-chopped. The lathe that I had originally wasn't big enough to swing the block so I had to do it by hand.

"I guess I have made approximately 20,000 decoys. That is just a guess. I really don't know.

Top center clockwise: Full-size Black Duck sleeper, Mallard drake, Canvasback hen, Green-winged Teal drake, Canvasback drake and Mallard hen made by Pat Vincenti.

View of the loft upstairs shows turned bodies of the different species to be made by Mr. Vincenti.

"A lot of the guys who used to help me make my decoys are making their own today. Dave Walker, Butch Wagoner, Johnny Clark, and Joey Jobes to name a few.

"My customers are mainly collectors. There are a few people who gun them but mainly they are collectors. We ship all across the country and the world. We have shipped to Portugal, Spain, Germany, New Zealand, Australia, England. Everywhere. How these people found out we will never know. I imagine it might be local people sending them.

"I started waterfowl hunting on the Flats with some of the boys I went to school with. After I got out of school we got our own rig together, bought the boats and made the decoys till we had several thousand dollars tied up in equipment. We were in junior high school when we started. I guess we all hunted together until about six or seven years ago. I hunted a lot with Butch Wagoner, Lenny Ferguson, Larry Morris, and John Clark. Body-booting was our main style. We killed a lot of birds body-booting, mostly geese. The ducks had pretty much left here by then. There were still some ducks around, but not like they talked about in the old days. I quit hunting about three or four years ago. The birds aren't here like they used to be and I don't have the time.

"My favorite species of duck are the Canvasback and the Swan. They are the simplest but I think they do the nicest.

"For hunting I guess my favorite was the Canada Goose. I like shooting ducks more than I like shooting geese but never really had much of an opportunity to hunt for ducks much.

"I've had about 3 or 4 gunning dogs, all Chesapeakes. They were all great dogs. This last one I have is smarter than I am. I've had him about eight years now.

"Every day we were out on that water was a memorable day to me. The company had a lot to do with it. We didn't have to kill a lot of birds either. We just had a good time. I do remember the night we were locked up. The water had froze up on the Flats and the geese were using one spot down off the western shore, right off of the Tydings property every night. The geese were going to the same spot every night and resting. The area the geese were using was about the size of several football fields and was stained brown and white from the geese.

"We decided we were going to go out there and lay in the same area and wait on them. There was 21 of us. We put a few decoys out and laid right on the ice. We were wearing white painters coveralls. It was just about quitting time and no geese had flown yet. We figured we were there and we were going to stay until they came. It was dark when the first goose came across the tree rows and way after quitting time. After the first goose came the whole flock came behind him. It was so dark you could see the fire coming out of the end of the guns. We had shot into a couple of bunches and were picking up our stuff and getting the geese together when a helicopter came. The pilot

Pat Vincenti and John Clark are picking up the full body Canada Goose decoys on the "Flats" after body-booting. The decoys were made by Pat and Mickey McMullen. Pat gives credit to Mr. McMullen who was the first to make the styrofoam full body with epoxy and wood chips.

turned the big search light on. He informed us that he was the Maryland State Police and that we were all under arrest, and that we were to proceed to Tydings Yacht Basin and not to try to get off the ice between there and the park because they were watching us. We just thought it was a big joke and got all our stuff together and went back to the park.

"Sure enough there they were, the State Police, the Maryland State Game Wardens and Havre de Grace town police, all waiting for us. You would have thought we had robbed Maryland National Bank or something. As we were coming off the ice in a single file they informed us that they wanted all the geese in one pile, all the guns in another pile, and all the licence in another pile. The only thing in our favor was that they really couldn't prove what time we had started shooting the geese. In other words, they couldn't say for sure we had killed some of the geese before or after dark. When we got into court the Game Warden told the judge that we had fired several rounds after quitting time. The judge asked the warden how many times. One time, two times, how many times did we shoot? The Game Warden told the judge, 'Your Honor, it sounded like a war. I don't know how many times they shot.' They really couldn't prove it was us. We got a year probation as far as game laws go, and fined $50.00 court costs. Actually we had come off the ice legal. Everybody had their limit. Everybody had three geese. But, you will have days like that, I guess.

"We had days when we would kill geese and days when we wouldn't kill any. Days when we never fired a gun, never saw any geese. I have seen days when the geese would come in at the decoys and your gun would be so full of ice that it wouldn't shoot. I've had days where my hands were so cold that I couldn't even pull a trigger on a gun. There were days when you would no sooner get set up when the tide would come in so fast it would be too deep for you to hunt. Other times I've seen days when the tide would go out so fast that your decoys would be sitting on sandy bottom.

"The only way to gun was body-booting on the Flats. It was a lot of work. We had four boats all the time. I'd go today just to get away for a while. I'm tickled to death just to sit in the pits. It doesn't make any difference whether I kill any birds anymore. I never thought I would see the day when it wouldn't bother me whether I killed a bird or not. I've seen days when we would kill a hundred and got mad because one flew away. It's really funny how it hits you. Today I don't care whether I fire a gun or not. I just like going to watch the birds.

"I owe just about all of my success to five guys. They are Madison Mitchell, Jimmy Pierce, Paul Gibson, Ed Sampson, and "Titbird" Bauer.

"I do collect birds, mostly Canvasbacks. I prefer the upper bay style of ducks. I still have the first decoy I ever bought from Mr. Mitchell. It was a hen Pintail. I made a lamp out of it in school. It was the only duck left in his hearse garage. All the racks were empty so I bought it. I only paid $3.00 for it."

Gilmore "Butch" Wagoner

"I was born in 1947 in Havre de Grace. I had finished thirteen years of schooling when I got a job with the Department of Defense. I'm an artillery repair inspector.

"Back in 1964 or 1965 I first started out using old bleach bottles for decoys. Later Joe Merkler and myself made silhouettes of a duck body out of a two-by-six. Then we would make a head out of a two-by-four and nail it on the two-by-six. The duck was attached to the flat side of another two-by-six for the flat bottom and ballast it needed to float.

"After serving time in the army in 1969 I started working with Jimmy Pierce in July of 1971. I worked there for about a year. One day I went down to Mr. Mitchell's shop and asked for a job. He told me he didn't have any jobs open. I told him that I would work for nothing if he would show me how to make decoys. I continued to work there till he sold the shop to Bill Collins. I learned everything there except painting the bodies and feathering. At that time Mr. Mitchell and 'Titbird' did the painting. "

"My decoys have been influenced by Mr. Mitchell and Jimmy Pierce since I started. Jimmy learned from him also. Lately I have been watching Charlie Joiner work. I am starting to learn that style in my painting. I'm also making some flat bottom gunning decoys, getting away the round bottom in some species.

"I prefer cedar if you can find it. Secondly, I'll use white pine or old barn wood or bass wood. All of the heads are glued on with a two part epoxy and covered with three coats of sealer. Rustoleum is used for body paint. I mix my colors just the way Madison taught me. Sixty percent oil, and forty percent japan colors. This will give you a satin type finish.

"In 1980 my decoy machine was made by myself and a friend from Delaware. I can turn out decoys from as large as a swan down to a duck. My wife has always helped me with the decoys. She band saws heads out, sands and putties. I call her a 'Preparation Technician.' My nephew helps also when he is not in school.

"I have at least four customers who buy Blackheads, Redheads, Canvasbacks and Pintails to gun over. They will gun over them for two years then sell them. This way they can make more money than it cost to buy new ones.

Gilmore "Butch" B. Wagoner puts the eye on a Pintail drake.

"I started hunting with my father in 1960 for rabbits and squirrels. In 1964 I started waterfowl hunting. I tried bushwhacking several times with Butch Ward, but we were not very famous at it. Body-booting was the main style of gunning I did. We had a combination rig between myself, Butch Ward, Butch Ferguson and Pat Vincenti. We had some great hunts back around 1966. One time we were done hunting geese and were back at the pier by eight-thirty in the morning."

Left front clockwise: full-size Green-winged Teal hen, Canvasback drake sleeper, Common Goldeneye hen, Common Goldeneye drake, Canvasback hen sleeper and Green-winged Teal drake made by Butch Wagoner.

David "Dave" Walker paints Bufflehead hen. Other decoys top left to right: Northern Shoveler drake, Northern Shoveler hen and Bufflehead drake.

David "Dave" Walker

"I was born September 10, 1958 in Havre de Grace, Maryland. I finished high school and my full-time profession is a machinist.

"My aunt gave me one of Jimmy Pierce's decoys when I was about fourteen years old. I believe it was a drake Canvasback. I wanted a hen so I went down to Jimmy's and started working. Just sanding and puttying for him. He knew I had an interest in decoy making so he let me help out at his shop. The funny thing is I never did get my hen.

"When I was about fifteen years old I began going to Jimmy Pierce's shop. I worked there for a couple of years and then, in 1975, I went to work for Madison Mitchell.

"My style of decoy making is a little bit of all three of the decoy makers I have worked with. That would be Mitchell, Pierce, and Jobes. But if I were pinned down I would have to say that it leans more towards Mitchell's style in both carving and painting.

"The woods I use are primarily white pine, white cedar and polonium. Primarily the white pine because it is more readily available.

"My paints are flat Rustoleum. I put a little bit of linseed oil in the paint. It kind of toughens it up a little bit and puts a little shine on it.

"My decoys are all machine made. I use the standard tools that most carvers use. That is spoke shave, draw knife, drum sander, belt sander and whittling knife. I have never hand-chopped any.

"If I had to make a guess I would say that I have made about 7,000 decoys so far.

"There are several people who were a big help to me. I never employed them as such, but they were a big help. They are Dave Sinclair, Carrie Christley, Carl Wheeler and James McFadden. Dave Sinclair and Carl Wheeler are making decoys on their own now.

"As time passed I learned to become a little neater in carving and to take extra care in the painting. No major style changes or patterns. I

Left front clockwise: full-size Pintail hen sleeper, Northern Shoveler drake, highneck Canvasback hen, highneck Canvasback drake, Northern Shoveler hen and American Widgeon (Baldpate) made by Dave Walker.

strive to keep the same style that Madison Mitchell did. That is, I make a round bottom decoy and the paint is such that a gunner can throw it in the water and not scare the birds away. But at the same time, because of the way I paint, you can also put them on the shelf.

"People collect my decoys for various reasons. I have quite a few gunners from North Carolina and Virginia who buy mainly Mallards and Black Ducks.

"When I gun I like to shoot Teal because they are so damned fast that they are hard to hit. Four of us went to Louisiana last November and hunted for four days. We did manage to kill quite a few of them. We pulled the boat up into the reeds and sat there along with the alligators.

"One of my more memorable hunts was shooting geese on the Eastern Shore with my father, Dan Finey, Kyle Eldrith, and Dave Thompson. We had a real good morning. We killed our limit, which, at that time, was three. We had to give up the farm on the shore. It has just gotten too expensive.

"When I worked down at Mitchell's I used to enjoy the different stories that the old-timers would tell. I remember one that Mitchell would tell us. When Madison was about 14 or 15 years old he used to help deliver milk. In the winter the milk was always frozen and it would stick up about an inch or so above the bottle. He would scrape it off and eat it. One morning this guy caught him and said, 'No wonder I haven't been getting a full bottle.' Mr. Mitchell said to him, 'Well, you don't want your cat licking on the bottle do you?' As if to say he was taking it off so that the cat wouldn't get to the bottle.

"Another thing I will never forget is Mr. Mitchell telling me politely that he was going to 'kick me in the bumper' if I ever did something not to his liking. But it was always said with that tone of voice which was serious but at the same time very kind."

Milton J. Watson
Born: 1911 lived in Chesapeake City, Cecil County, Maryland
Died: 1985

J. Milton Watson stands next to his decoy machine he called "The Beaver."

Full-size highneck Canvasback hen made by Milton Watson.

Full-size highneck Canvasback drake made by Mr. Watson.

Painted Swan background is the door of Mr. Watson's shop.
On top step, Full-size Whistling (Tundra) Swan, Bottom step,
Canvasback hen and Canvasback drake made by Mr. Watson.

Clarence Webb, Jr. paints on Redhead hen. Wood Duck drake sits on table.

Clarence Webb

"I was born Oct 8, 1906 in Kent County, Maryland, the town of Fairlee. When I was 7 years old we moved to Cecil County. I was born on a farm and worked on different farms till the forties.

"I made my first decoys in 1955 out of cedar post. They were round bottom black heads. I made fifty-five Canvasbacks to add to the ones I had bought and used them in my bushwhacking rig on the Susquehanna flats. I designed them off of Heverin's somewhat, but I made the bodies wider and longer. The bigger decoy seemed to ride better in rough water then the smaller ones. I felt they looked more natural to the ducks.

"In later years I decided to make a few other species to gun over. I've made Pintails, Redheads, Teal and Wood Ducks. I made my own patterns and had Mr. Madison Mitchell turn the bodies for me since I never owned a machine. A draw knife and spoke shave were used to smooth the body. White pine was preferred for the bodies and heads.

"Oil and lead paints were used until they outlawed the lead paint. Then I painted with Rustoleum. I never made a lot of decoys, maybe four to five hundred in all. I sold a few but not for gunning stools, just collectors. I haven't been able to climb up the stairs over the garage in several years, so I haven't made any decoys since then.

"Hunting was a big part of my life. I started when I was fourteen years old on the farm. In the thirties I was the manager of a farm owned by Mr. Ruley Carpenter, whose son was Bob Carpenter. Ruley Carpenter was a conservationist, he never shot over the limit and never allowed alcohol in the blind. We used to use live decoys back in those days up till 1935 when they were outlawed. I made goose silhouettes realistic looking with the painting and put them out in a way that looked natural for the geese. I can decoy just as many geese with silhouettes as you can with mounted birds. I called by mouth because I never found a caller that would suit me, they were all too high pitched.

"I only remember one time that we never killed a goose, it was foggy day and nothing flew. We might not kill the limit every time but we did manage to get a few. I always obeyed the bag limits when I hunted, and never killed over the limit. However, when I was a boy I night-gunned with a couple other boys a few times.

"I caught a cripple goose that had been grazed across the eye and head. I used him for many years along with about thirty other live decoys. When you used live decoys you didn't need any other type of decoys. You put a string around the breast with a snap. Then you snap a line with a little more weight than a wood decoy to hold them in one area. They would just swim around and call, you can't beat that for being natural."

Top, full-size Wood Duck drake. Bottom, Wood Duck hen made by Clarence Webb.

Charles T. Wilson
Born: unknown lived in Havre de Grace, Harford County, Maryland
Died: unknown

Canvasback drake made by Charles T. Wilson.

Glossary

Baiting—The illegal use of bait such as dried corn or wheat in the water or on the ground to attract waterfowl close enough to shoot.

Body booting—Hunting where the hunter wears chest waders or dry diving suit to keep themselves dry while standing in the water, sometimes up to their chest. Full body and V-board goose and duck decoys are set out. Stickups attached to eight foot pipe, one for each hunter are spaced safely apart in the decoys. The stickups can be turned in 360 degrees to hide the hunter from approaching waterfowl.

Booby blind—A wooden blind that stands out in the water from shore. Some have long walk ways or necessitate the use of a boat to reach them.

Bushwhack boat—A wooden boat sixteen to twenty feet long that was painted white. The front had white cloth attached to wood stakes that attached to the boat. This helped to conceal the hunters as they approached the ducks. The boat was sculled during the approach to the decoys. There was almost no noise while sculling and no movement to disturb the ducks.

Bushwhacking—A style of hunting waterfowl from a boat. Decoys are set out. The boat is rowed up wind several hundred yards from the decoys. The hunters watch as the ducks land into their decoys. Then they scull the boat into the decoys and shoot as the ducks leave the water.

Cans—Canvasback Ducks

Cripples—Waterfowl that has been crippled when shot, injured but not killed. Also a term for heavily used decoys in need of repair and repaint.

Crowbills, Mud Hen, Coot—A duck known as the American Coot.

Dart—A flock of ducks or geese passing through the decoys.

Decoy Machine—A machine that resembles a wood lathe, which is used to turn out round bottom decoy bodies. Custom-designed and made by the decoy maker.

Draw knife—A wood-shaping tool

Drum sander—A sanding machine which uses a round rubber drum mounted on a electric motor shaft. A sandpaper sleeve fits over drum. A rubber drum is then inflated to tighten paper sleeve.

Flagging—Waving a black cloth attached to a stick, real goose wings, or plastic, wood, or cardboard shaped wings painted flat black to attract geese to the decoys. Geese seem to be used to movement in a flock geese on the ground, and therefore are not disturbed by this movement. It appears to work best on bright sunny days.

Full body decoys—A decoy that shows all the dimensions of the intended species.

Gunning stool—The hunter's spread of decoys

Jelutong—Wood from Malaysia used in making decoys because it is easily carved.

Junk yard rig—A decoy spread consisting of automobile tires and silhouettes. The use of over one thousand decoys in a spread is not uncommon.

"Natures Grace" Whistling (Tundra) Swan.

Layout boat—A layout boat can only be used in certain waters in Maryland. The boat must be eighteen inches high at the sides. These usually can conceal four hunters at one time. Silhouette decoys are attached to the sides to help conceal the hunters.

Layout rig—Consists of V-boards, full body decoys, and a layout boat. Decoys are set out and layout boat is anchored in the widest spread of the decoys.

Pass shooting—The hunting of waterfowl in an area that is known for their frequent travel. A blind is set up, usually in a hedge row that waterfowl pass over at low altitudes.

Paulownia—A light weight wood that is easy to carve. A native of China, it grows from New York to Florida to Texas.

Pit—A wooden blind that is placed below the ground level. It is then covered with natural cover such as corn stalks to conceal hunters.

Shore blind—A wooden blind that is located next to the water's edge. It can be reached by walking.

Silhouette Decoy—Decoys made of plywood or masonite. Metal rod is fastened to plywood to be pushed into the ground, holding the decoy upright.

Sinkbox—A coffin-like box with a floating flexible platform attached to all four sides. The sink box with gunner was weighted so that it appeared to be level with the water. Four to six hundred decoys were set out around the sink box. The gunner would lay back in the box and was actually below the surface of the water. The gunner would sit up to shoot when ducks were over the decoys.

Spoke shave—A wood-shaping tool.

Sprig tail—Pintail Ducks

Stickup—A large, oversized silhouette of a goose made from plywood. A stickup is fastened to a metal pipe that is pushed into the river bottom so that it is close to the water and conceals the hunter. On the back of the stickup is a rack for a shotgun and a small shelf to hold shotgun shells.

Tire decoys—A used glass-belted car tire is cut into three equal pieces. The pieces are then turned inside out. This spreads the tire open and allows it to stand on its own. A slot is cut for the insertion a wooden head. Some hunters paint the tire to be more realistic.

Toll—A flight of waterfowl landing in the decoys.

V-Boards or Frames—A silhouette decoy fastened to a wooden stick approximately three to four feet long. Three of these are used to make one V-board. The three sticks are then attached to a hinge that allows the sticks to form a triangle. A lead weight is then attached to the V-board by way of a strong cord to keep the V-board from floating away. V-boards, when folded, take up little room compared to full body decoys and can be stacked.

Whittling Knife—Large wood handled knife with a blade usually made from a straight razor.

Museums

Havre de Grace Decoy Museum

Havre de Grace, Maryland is known as the "Decoy Capital of the World." Decoys have been produced in countless numbers from the numerous makers of this area for almost two centuries.

On November 2, 1986 the Havre de Grace Decoy Museum opened its doors to the public. Since that time visitors from all fifty states and thirty countries have passed through.

On display you will find some of the finest decoys of the area. There is a wet display featuring a sinkbox which was outlawed in the early thirties. There are demonstrations of decoy making and many other artifacts pertaining to the hunting of waterfowl.

In the fall of 1989 the second level addition is expected to open. The museum is located off US Route 40 in Havre de Grace, Maryland.

Upper Bay Museum

Upper Bay Museum in North East, Maryland is located on the North East River. The museum was started in June of 1981. The building was know as Harvey's Fish House and is over one hundred years old. Visitors will find a great assortment of historic items from this area.

Displays cover the history from the market hunters to the watermen. Decoys, sinkboxes, bushwhack boats, rail bird skiffs and big gun skiffs are just a few of the items. There is one of the finest collections of outboard boat motors in existence located here.

The Upper Bay Museum is located in Cecil County, Maryland. Follow Maryland Route 272 one South of U.S. Route 40 intersection to Walnut Street and the North East Community Park.

Upper Eastern Shore decoy shed holds thousands of silhouettes, V-boards and floating decoys. Left clockwise: Master guide Floyd Price, guide Paul Wilks, guide Tom Geist and guide Mike Bradway.